Humanism and/or Behaviorism in Education

Walter B. Kolesnik

Humanism and/or Behaviorism in Education

Walter B. Kolesnik
University of Detroit

ALLYN AND BACON, INC.
BOSTON

TO KATHRYN

Library of Congress Cataloging in Publication Data

Kolesnik, Walter Bernard, 1923-
    Humanism and/or behaviorism in education.

    Bibliography: p.
    1. Educational psychology.   2. Behavior modification.   3. School discipline   I. Title.
LB1051.K723   370.15   74-16445

Contents

Preface

Humanism and behaviorism are without doubt the two dominant psychological theories in contemporary education. Practically every method of teaching and pattern of curriculum organization is based on one or another or both of these systems. So are the vast majority of educational innovations that have been tried in recent years and reforms that are currently being proposed. Each of these two psychologies is rooted in philosophical principles that are pertinent to most of the classroom problems that most teachers face. To a very great extent, the direction that education takes in the years to come will depend on which of these two theories is implemented or on the manner in which they might be reconciled.

Numerous books advocating either humanistic or behavioristic education are available, but I know of none that attempts to relate them as this one does. This book presents in one nontechnical, unbiased, easy-to-read source a comparison of humanism and behaviorism as they pertain to education. The first chapter draws attention to some of the major problems and issues in education and examines a dozen or more criticisms of our schools; the rest of the book relates behaviorism and humanism to these issues and criticisms. The second chapter summarizes the basic principles and assumptions of humanism. The third deals with the educational implications of humanistic psychology and the kinds of practices that humanistic educators recommend. Chapter four presents an overview of the principles and assumptions of behavioral psychology. Chapter five is concerned with the implications of, and recommendations based on, that system. Chapter six attempts to help the readers synthesize the two apparently conflicting positions and to integrate what they might perceive as the more attractive features of each.

I have tried to present the two theories and their implications fairly, concisely, objectively, and sympathetically. While my own feelings and interpretations do occasionally intrude, I have permitted them to do so only minimally in an attempt to provide a balanced view of "both sides." My purpose, in short, has not been to propagate my views but rather to help readers formulate their own conclusions about education, behaviorism, and humanism.

This book is primarily intended for prospective teachers of educational psychology, foundations of education, and philosophy of education courses. It presupposes no previous work in any of these areas. Advanced students and experienced teachers might find some of the material familiar, but the book is also intended to serve them as a refresher, a basis for discussion, and a stimulus for thinking about some of our more pressing educational problems.

Walter B. Kolesnik

1

Schools

They Can't Be All That Bad

If there's one thing this world of ours has plenty of it's problems. There is, for example, the perennial problem of wars and how to prevent them. Then there is the problem of poverty, especially in the midst of affluence. There are the problems of racial and ethnic tensions, of hatred and intolerance, and of man's well-known inhumanity to his fellow man. There are the problems of air and water pollution, the depletion of our natural resources, and the resultant or threatened deterioration in the "quality of life" to which we have become accustomed. There are the problems of the nation's health and the needs of our old people.

There are also the problems of urban decay and suburban indifference, of corruption in and distrust of government, of organized crime and crime on the streets, of unemployment and the high cost of living. There are the problems of alcoholism and drug addiction and suicides and venereal disease, of unhappy marriages and unwanted, if not abused, children, and a great many other social and economic and political and moral problems growing out of technology or the population explosion or changing sex roles or changing patterns of family life or changing heaven knows what.

As though these were not enough, each of us also has his personal or emotional or psychological problems. We all have, to a greater or lesser degree, our own private fears, conflicts, frustrations, and anxieties. We are all striving to satisfy our needs for love and esteem and self-fulfillment. But we do not always succeed. We continue to search for an identity, for a set of values to live by, for something that will give meaning to our existence. But sometimes that search seems endless.

2

All of these problems, as I perceive them, have at least this much in common: they are all basically educational problems. If they are ever going to be solved, their solutions will have to depend, more than anything else, on what individual human beings know and believe and are able to do and want to do. If they are not solved or even alleviated in our lifetimes, we will have to live with them and try to make the best of things. How happy and successful each of us is in this effort will depend to a great extent on the knowledge and skills, values and beliefs, abilities and aspirations he has acquired through the process known as education.

EDUCATION AND SCHOOLING

By the term education I do not necessarily mean schooling. And I certainly do not wish to imply that schools, in and of themselves, can be counted on to end wars, stop pollution, solve the crime problem or transform unhappy into happy people. Schools are only one source, and not necessarily the most important source, of a person's knowledge, skills, attitudes, values, beliefs, and his ways of learning, thinking, feeling, and otherwise behaving. Other sources include one's family and friends, church, communication and entertainment media, and business organizations, to name a few. The sum total of one's education may be, and probably is, more attributable to such "informal" educational agencies than to the things he learned in school.

A number of reputable studies have shown, for example, that a person's political views, religious beliefs, attitudes toward various social and political issues, and his moral standards are not nearly so dependent on his schooling as they are on what he learned elsewhere, particularly from his parents, brothers and sisters, friends and close associates. There is also good reason to believe that television, books and magazines and newspapers, films and records are far more instrumental than schools in

3

shaping individuals' attitudes, values, tastes, and goals. A case has even been made that such things as one's income as an adult, the success of his marriage, and his overall happiness and personal adjustment are more directly attributable to nonschool than to school learning experiences.

Without belaboring the point we might simply note a few of the many other things we have learned, not through formal systematic instruction in school, but casually, incidentally, informally in situations outside the school: how to speak and understand our native language; how to feed and clothe ourselves; who our friends are; where to buy a good used car; what to do with our spare time; which politician to trust; how to find our way around town; when to turn the TV set on and when to turn it off; what to do with our money if we have any and how to get some if we don't; how we feel about our neighbors; how we feel about ourselves.

The distinction between formal and informal education is certainly worth noting, but equating them respectively with schooling and extra schooling is not quite valid. Some of the things a person learns in school, such as his attitudes toward literature or his feelings about his fellow students or himself, are usually not formally taught, but are learned concomitantly, incidentally, and perhaps unconsciously. At the same time, some of the things he learns from his parents or friends or from a television commentator or a film producer may be the consequence of formal, deliberate attempts at teaching, perhaps even in the sense of indoctrination. So formal education and schooling, informal education and nonschooling, do not always or necessarily go together.

In the pages that follow we will be particularly concerned with that part of the total educational process that takes place in, or is at least directly related to, the institutions we call schools. As a tentative, working definition, we can think of education as the life-long process by which a person assimilates his cultural heritage, that is, the process by which he acquires whatever it is that previous generations have found necessary or desirable for survival or success in his particular environment.

The word heritage implies a passing down from generation to generation of the accumulated experiences of the past. The word cultural implies the knowledge, traditions, beliefs—in short, the way of life—of a particular society. As we shall see, not everyone accepts this concept of education, but it will do nicely for our present purposes.

Historically, schools were established in order to transmit, rather formally and systematically, those parts of the culture which an individual could not acquire as readily, or at all, from his casual everyday experiences. Some of these specialized and relatively complex aspects of the heritage came to be organized into bodies of knowledge known as subject matter, or into skills such as reading and writing, critical thinking and problem solving. Other aspects are referred to as attitudes, appreciations, customs, values, etc. Probably most, but certainly not all, people still consider the school's main function to be that of transmitting such aspects of their culture.

SOME PROBLEMS AND ISSUES

Thus far we have suggested what at first might seem to be a rather sweeping assumption: that the happiness of individuals, the welfare of their societies, and even the alleviation of major world problems depend on the process of education. We have also suggested that schools alone cannot be expected to, because they are not intended to and are not equipped to, provide for all of a person's education. Still the school is the one institution that has been officially charged with the responsibility for filling some of his educational needs. But which ones?

There is nowhere near universal agreement about what the schools should be doing or why or how they should be doing it. Among the questions being asked and debated, not only by professional educators but by many members of the general public as well, are the following: Why do we have schools in the first place? Whatever their historical antecedents might be, why do we tax ourselves to maintain public schools and require young people, often against their will, to attend them? Are there viable alternatives to our present system of formal education? Might it be that compulsory school attendance laws are obsolete? Might there be more effective ways of achieving the purpose of education, whatever those purposes might be?

Do our schools exist primarily for the sake of the individual student or for the good of society? Should our schools focus on developing the student's "individuality" or on preparing him to take his place in the established social order? Is there a difference between the concept of education as the production of "good citizens" and that of education as the development of free and happy individuals? If so, with which should our schools be particularly concerned? If not, what can the schools do to resolve the apparent difference?

Are there certain bodies of knowledge that everyone should be required to learn in order to become a good citizen or a free and happy individual or both? If so, what are these subjects and why are they so vital? Should all children and young people be expected to learn pretty much the same thing at the same rate and to the same degree? Or should each pupil decide for himself what and when and how much he will attempt to learn? Or should the school administration try to individualize the educational program by setting up different requirements and procedures for each?

Should our students be allowed more freedom in planning and carrying out their own educational programs and in regulating their own school behavior, or is there perhaps a need for even stricter rules and regulations, requirements and controls? Have our schools been needlessly regimenting their students, perhaps to the point of oppression, forcing them into patterns of conformity in order to satisfy the desires of the adult authority structure? Or have they been too lax and permissive? Or are they "about right" in this respect?

Everyone agrees that we want and need "good" teachers, but what do we mean by "good" in this context? How can we identify and reward excellent teachers or distinguish those who

6

are mediocre from those who are inadequte or totally ineffective? To what extent, if any, should teachers be held "accountable" for their students' failures to learn? What, in short, do we expect our teachers to be or to do?

Should teaching be regarded as a kind of creative art, calling for a great deal of imagination, spontaneity, and improvisation? Or should it be thought of more as a science or a branch of human engineering, with a prescribed systematic methodology to be rather scrupulously observed?

How useful are such traditional incentives as grades and report card marks and the competitiveness which they seem to imply? Are there other incentives that might be more effective? Or should teachers abandon the carrot and stick approach to motivation and concentrate more on trying to make school work interesting? If they do the latter, should they rely more on the student's existing interests and help him learn what he wants to learn? Or should the teacher try to arouse and maintain the student's interest in the material she wants him to learn.*

What is the responsibility of the school with respect to the student's moral formation or his character development? Should the school attempt to transmit and inculcate certain predetermined attitudes, values, beliefs, and moral principles? Or should it encourage each student to formulate his own value system and moral code? Or should it perhaps refuse to let itself be drawn into this controversial, emotionally-charged, and highly sensitive area, leaving the matter to the child's family or his church?

What about the student's mental health? Does the school have any particular responsibility with respect to his emotional development? What, if anything, can and should the school do,

---

*Throughout this book I will be using feminine pronouns to refer to teachers and masculine pronouns for students. There is, of course, nothing feminine about teaching or masculine about learning. My choice of pronouns is purely arbitrary, intended solely for purposes of clarity and consistency in communication. The expression "his or her" is awkward, especially when used repeatedly. To refer to a teacher (or a student) as "he" in one sentence and "she" in another might be needlessly confusing.

or attempt to do, in order to reduce students' feelings of inferiority or guilt or hostility or alienation? What can the school do to develop the individual's self-confidence and feeling of personal worth? How can it help satisfy his social needs and contribute to his developing a positive self-concept? Or is this sort of thing really no great concern of the schools at all?

If you are looking for nice, neat, simple, little definitive answers to questions such as these, you are looking in the wrong place. You will not find them in this book and I doubt that you will find them in any other. But if you would like to clarify your own thinking on some of these problems and issues and eventually come up with some defensible positions of your own, keep reading.

CRITICISMS OF THE SCHOOLS

No one knows precisely when or where the first "school" was established; it depends on your definition of a school. But it would be a safe bet that fifteen minutes after the first school came into existence, at least a few critics were already pecking away at it. From at least as far back as the time of the ancient Greeks onward, the history of education has been replete with allegations that the schools were not doing a particularly good job. For centuries there have been those who had, or thought they had, a better idea of how the young should be educated, of what and how and why they should be taught. So criticisms of schools and recommendations for educational reform are certainly nothing new.

Since the middle of the present century, however, such criticisms seem to have been more intense and persistent than ever before. Undoubtedly they have been more widespread. Hardly a day has gone by in the last couple of decades without some newspaper or magazine article, some television show or radio program, some author or lecturer or educator or legislator or parent or student proclaiming the deficiencies of the educa-

8

tional system and its need for (often drastic) reform. Let's take a quick overview of some of the more common of these criticisms. Whether or not they are fair is a decision you will have to make for yourself. So is the judgment as to which, if any, of the recommended changes would constitute an improvement over, and not simply an alteration of, the existing situation.

ROMANTIC CRITICS — humanists

One of the most widely-quoted contemporary educational critics has been Charles Silberman. Especially widely-quoted is a statement from his best-seller, *Crisis in the Classroom*, to the effect that schools are "grim, joyless, intellectually sterile places that kill dreams and mutilate minds." He believes that they should be pleasant, happy, intellectually stimulating places that develop minds and help people realize their dreams. This is essentially the position of John Holt, Herbert Kohl, Neil Postman, Charles Weingartner, Jonathan Kozol, Carl Rogers, George Leonard and others who have been referred to as romantics, and whose ideas have been derived from humanistic psychology. Some of their books and others in a similar vein are included in the bibliography. In this chapter I shall be referring to critics such as these as romantics or humanists, using the terms interchangeably, simply for the sake of variety.

All of the so-called romantic reformers or humanistic educators do not, of course, agree among themselves in every detail as to exactly how formal education should be changed. But they are certainly in agreement that change is necessary and long overdue. They believe that the kinds of problems mentioned at the beginning of this chapter can be solved—through education. But not through education as they presently find it. The kinds of changes they urge center around such concepts as freedom, informality, flexibility, spontaneity, joy, and above all, individuality.

According to humanistic psychology, the purpose of education is not simply to teach subject matter or to convey information or to "transmit the cultural heritage." Its purpose most certainly is not to program students to make predetermined responses or to fit them into any predetermined mold or to transform a particular student into a replica of someone else. The purpose of education, humanists maintain, is to help develop the individuality of each and every student, to develop his potentialities whatever they might be, to help him become to the fullest extent possible what he is capable of becoming: an authentic, autonomous, self-actualizing, happy human being.

FAILURE TO INDIVIDUALIZE

A perennial criticism of formal education, but one that has been emphasized in recent years, especially, though not exclusively, by humanistic educators, is the failure of schools to individualize. If there is one indisputable principle in the entire realm of educational psychology, it is the truism that no two people are identical; that individuals differ from one another, often significantly, in just about every observable way possible: in their abilities, interests, problems, needs, goals; in their racial, ethnic, socioeconomic, religious, and family backgrounds; in the ways they develop; in the ways they learn, the rates at which they learn, in what they want to learn, and in what they need to learn.

Despite these well-known and rather obvious differences, and despite the great amount of experimentation and the many innovative programs intended to provide for them, critics maintain that all students in a particular class are still likely to be treated as though they were all pretty much alike, expected, if not required, to learn much the same thing in the same way within the same time span. Such devices as a broad array of electives and mini-courses, nongraded classrooms, flexible modular scheduling, "open" classrooms, work-study programs, the use of learning centers, community resources and paraprofessionals, and individualized projects are perceived by the romantics as steps in the right direction. But they are likely to reject some of the other means that have been used to try to individualize instruction, such as teaching machines, contracts, computer assisted instruction, individually prescribed instructional programs, and even attempts at homogeneous grouping, on the grounds that these do not really individualize, but are only techniques for programming students more efficiently.

The ideal of humanistic educators is a school where each student would set his own objectives, plan his own particular course of study, decide what he wants to learn and when and how to learn it. He would proceed in his own way at his own pace without comparisons to what anyone else is doing. When he decided it was time to do so, he would evaluate his own work in terms of his own standards. The romantics find that very few American schools are anywhere near this ideal, but that most of them operate more in accordance with a mass-production, assembly-line model.

PETTY, OPPRESSIVE RULES

Another common romantic criticism of our schools is that they are characterized by far too many petty and oppressive rules and requirements. Recognizing that some regulations of student behavior might be necessary, the romantics complain that too many of our schools have too many regulations dealing with trivial points that reflect the whims of teachers or administrators but serve no useful educational purpose whatsoever. Teachers and administrators, they claim, are often more concerned with peace and quiet, order and control, lesson plans and syllabi, timetables and record-keeping than they are with children or education. Consequently, the system is governed by schedules, bells and "periods" designed for the convenience of school officials, but having little if anything to do with learning. They point out, by way of example, that in more than one

11

instance, a lively discussion or an interesting and exciting lesson has had to be terminated abruptly because a bell rang, signalling the students to move to another room to take up another subject about which, at that particular time, they could not have cared less.

What one teacher regards as a rule which is all but essential to the management of her class, another might, of course, perceive as arbitrary and needlessly restrictive. So everyone, I suppose, has his own list of what he regards as "petty, oppressive" rules. Among those mentioned frequently by the romantic critics are such things as dress and hair regulations, forbidding students to chew gum in class, requiring that they enter and leave the classroom in a prescribed manner, that they occupy an assigned seat and remain there until given permission to leave, that they maintain silence not only in the classroom but in the corridors and maybe even in the cafeteria as well, and that they are not even allowed to go to the toilet without first publicly indicating their need and receiving the teacher's permission.

John Holt contends that there are only four places where people are forced to remain and where they are deprived of their freedom and subjected to this kind of oppression: prisons, mental institutions, the armed forces, and schools. He is far from being alone in likening schools to jails or concentration camps. About the only kinds of rules they think necessary are those which keep the students from hurting one another. Just about anything beyond that, they regard as an infringement on the individual's freedom. And to the romantics the concept of freedom is as vital as that of individuality.

FEAR

A corollary of the criticism which has just been mentioned is the charge that our entire educational system is based to a considerable and undesirable degree on fear: fear of being punished for violating one of the rules, fear of failure, fear of low grades, fear of making mistakes, fear of not pleasing the teacher, fear of ridicule or humiliation or rejection for not doing what she expects even when it is not clear as to what exactly she does expect. The romantics maintain that schools not only use these fears but actually cultivate them, the better to control and manipulate students. Many teachers, they claim, want their students to be at least a bit afraid of them and often wish they were a lot more fearful than they are. While these fears do perhaps facilitate classroom management, they are also supposed to induce hostility, alienation, and rebellion in some students, passivity, docility, and timidity in others. They are supposed to weaken the student's ability and desire to learn. They are supposed to force him into a situation where he attempts to learn what for him might be the wrong things, in the wrong way, for the wrong reasons: to avoid the consequences of not learning, to get good report card marks or simply to get the teacher off his back.

For optimum learning to take place, humanistic psychologists insist, the child needs an emotionally comfortable atmosphere in which he can feel psychologically secure and as free as possible from unnecessary pressures, anxieties, and threats. Ideally, the atmosphere should be one in which he can pursue his natural tendencies to explore, investigate, experiment, take chances, and make mistakes, without fear of what his teacher's reaction might be. The school, in short, should be a pleasant place where the student wants to be because of the joyful experiences awaiting him there. It should be, but according to the romantic critics, it usually is not.

MUTUAL DISTRUST AND DISRESPECT

Romantic critics also find that teachers and their students all too often do not trust, or respect, or even like one another. Teachers, they charge, often perceive students not as friends to be helped but as adversaries, or potential adversaries, to be controlled. They assume that students are preoccupied with trying to get away with something and feel that it's their job to make sure they don't. Thus, a big part of the teacher's efforts involves checking up on students to find out what mischief they might be contemplating or what rules they have broken or what work they did not do or what they failed to remember from last week's lesson. Students, in turn, do become intent on finding ways to beat the system or put something over on the teacher or satisfy her with a minimum of exertion or somehow defeat her in the game they have been forced into playing—under her ground rules on her home field.

Effective teaching, according to humanistic psychology, is essentially an interpersonal relationship between an individual in need of help and one who is capable of and willing to provide it. It is a relationship characterized by open, positive feelings about one another and by mutual respect. Some teachers seem to labor under the impression that they deserve the respect of their students, and possibly their affection as well, simply because they have been certified by the state as teachers. What they may fail to realize, and what humanistic educators persist in trying to point out, is that they must earn this respect, and that the best, if not the only, way to do so is by first demonstrating a genuine respect for the students. But such respect the romantics frequently find lacking. What they all too often find instead is a "don't turn your back on the little bastards" attitude.

UNRELATED TO THE REAL WORLD

Much of the current criticism of American school systems has grown out of a concern for the education of so-called disadvantaged children and youth. Humanistically-inclined educators who taught in what they called slum schools discovered that conventional educational programs, designed for white middle-class students, were ill-suited to the needs of minority group students who were neither white nor middle class. Upon due consideration they concluded that the conventional curricula and methodologies were not all that good for the white middle-class kids either. The shibboleth of the romantics became relevance.

As they see it, today's schools constitute an artificial environment which has little if any correspondence to the world of reality outside its walls. In being confined to this unnatural environment, often against their wills, students are said to feel cut off from the main stream of life. In this make-believe world they are expected to learn material which they often find dull, boring, and lacking in applicability to their real problems, interests, and needs. If they don't, they may be branded stupid or lazy or uncooperative or failures. They are required to learn chunks of subject matter that do not even seem to be related to one another, much less to the world outside the school. They are told that these subjects are very important, but they are not told why. If they are, the reason given is that they will find the material useful sometime in the future. But for the students the time is now. Why, the romantics wonder, so much emphasis on preparing the child for the future, when life is going on at the present? The humanists maintain that children naturally want to learn, not necessarily the things their teachers want them to learn, but things that they feel will help them live better lives not only in the years to come but here and now. What the romantics dislike in this regard is not only the irrelevance (or uselessness) of much of the material taught in the schools for many of the students, but also the invisible wall that blocks the school out from the rest of the community. They dislike the notion that education is something that one gets in a school and that living is something that one does after school. They would prefer to see a much larger part of the child's formal education taking place outside the school and a lot more living, as opposed to preparation for living, inside.

Preparation for the future is, of course, a matter that cannot be dismissed quite so casually. And part of reality is the world of work. The criticism here is that many high school graduates, not to mention dropouts, are unable to find jobs and take their place in that world because they lack the necessary skills or competencies. The traditional educational program, even with its sprinkling of vocational courses, has apparently not been of much help to many young people in this respect. So, the critics contend, our schools are not only deficient in helping students live more fully in the real world of the present, but they have been something less than successful in their avowed purpose of helping them prepare for the future.

FAILURE TO PROMOTE INDEPENDENT THINKING

Just about everyone would agree that the schools have a major role to play in helping students learn how to engage in good independent thinking. Many would maintain that of all the school's responsibilities, this objective is by far the most important. But our romantic reformers believe that, for the most part, schools have not been particularly successful in this respect either. They maintain that in their preoccupation with filling the memories of students with miscellaneous bits of information, the schools have not only neglected the cultivation of students' higher mental processes, but have actually stifled the development of their critical and creative capacities. Thus, many people with high school diplomas, and for that matter with college degrees, are unable to make wise decisions or attack problems intelligently or manifest originality because they were never taught how, or, as a humanistic psychologist would prefer to put it, they were never given much in the way of opportunity and encouragement to learn how.

Most teachers probably have a verbal commitment to the goal of fostering independent thinking but, according to the critics, many do not want their students to question or challenge or criticize or try to improve on their own views. Students may actually be penalized for expressing interpretations different from those of the textbook or teacher, while uncritical acceptance and reproduction of those interpretations are rewarded. Particularly in sensitive, controversial areas, the critics find that students are sometimes inhibited from formulating and expressing their own opinions and pressured into going along with those of the majority, or at least pretending to. But even in noncontroversial matters such as a mathematical problem the teacher might decide that it's much simpler and quicker to give the student a conclusion than it is to have him arrive at it independently.

Humanistic educators are more concerned with the process of education than they are with its products. They believe that the schools should be less concerned with trying to teach students what to think, and more with helping them learn how to think—how to reach their own conclusions, make their own decisions, and solve their own problems. Toward this end they recommend allowing the students a great deal more freedom and a great many more opportunities to explore, investigate, experiment, discover, analyze, synthesize, evaluate, criticize, and create than they are likely to have in our traditional schools.

NEGLECT OF AFFECTIVE EDUCATION

The romantics are not so upset by students' low academic achievement, particularly as it is measured on standardized tests, as they are by the schools' alleged neglect of what has come to be called the affective dimension of education. Educational objectives are commonly classified under two main headings: cognitive and affective. Cognitive objectives are those which pertain to such intellectual processes as knowing, understanding, thinking, acquiring and retaining knowledge—processes with which our schools traditionally have been primarily concerned. Affective objectives pertain more to such subjective emotional processes as feeling, believing, liking or disliking; they have to do with one's attitudes, values, preferences, appreciations and the like.

According to humanistic psychology, the affective dimension might be, and often is, of greater consequence to the individual than the cognitive. For example, how a person feels about Mozart or the scientific method or the Bill of Rights or mathematics or premarital sex or Martin Luther King or China might be a lot more important than what he knows about them. Particularly significant, from the humanistic standpoint, are an individual's feelings or beliefs about, perceptions of, and attitudes toward himself. As part of one's cognitive education, a person might learn many things about himself and come to understand himself in an objective, scientific, intellectual sense. As part of his affective education, he might come to accept himself, like himself, value himself—or reject himself.

Affective education is often part of the so-called hidden curriculum. This refers to material which the teacher does not formally teach or intend to teach, which she might not even realize her students are learning, and which might not even be true, but which students do learn incidentally, informally, concomitantly. Through this hidden curriculum a student might learn, for example, that he is stupid, or troublesome, or worthless, or inferior, or bad, or a failure, or odd, or insignificant, or hopeless, or too dumb to bother with. He may be explicitly told these things, but even if he is not, this may be the message that comes through.

A student might, on the other hand, learn that he is loved, wanted, accepted by adults who have a genuine interest in his welfare and a strong desire to help him. He might learn that he has potentialities worth developing and that they can and will be developed. He might learn to have confidence in himself and that he has a good chance to amount to something. He might learn that he has a great deal of personal worth and that he is valued and respected by his peers as well as by those adults whom he regards as significant in his life.

18

Humanistic educators believe that one of the most important things a person learns in school is his self-concept. They complain that all too often students acquire concepts of themselves which are negative, unfavorable, and self-destructive. Moreover, they find that all too often instead of helping students with their personal, social, and emotional problems, certain school policies, practices, and pressures actually intensify such problems, lower the individual's self-esteem, contribute to his feelings of frustration, and induce feelings of guilt, hostility or alienation. The point here is that in the opinion of the romantic critics, schools do not pay as much attention to the affective elements, especially the student's feelings about himself, as they should, and that in some cases, by omission and thoughtlessness, if not by design, they have had detrimental effects on students' personality development.

THE CUSTODIAL HIGH SCHOOL

Especially under attack by some of the romantic reformers has been the American high school. As a means of helping young people make the transition from the dependency of childhood to the independence of adulthood and as a means of preparing them for mature, responsible citizenship, many of the humanistic types regard the traditional high school as pretty much a waste. For college preparatory purposes, they maintain, one year of high school or two at the most would be plenty if the colleges and high schools would only try to articulate their programs more closely, as a few have at least begun to do. For those who are not college bound, high school attendance is not only unnecessary for the welfare of the individual or the good of society, but they claim might actually do more harm than good. Many teenagers quite obviously do not like high school and do not want to attend. So, they ask, why force them? The main reason seems to be that adults in positions of authority believe that high school attendance is somehow good for a young person whether he realizes it or not. Perhaps a more honest reason, according to the reformers, is that there is nothing else for teenagers to do, no place else for them to go. They are not needed at home. They are not wanted on the employment market. Nobody wants them walking the streets. So they are sent to school. The high school, as a consequence, has become largely a custodial institution, something like a jail.

Confining the young person to this kind of custodial institution, it has been argued, has a number of detrimental effects on the individual's overall development. For one thing, it actually inhibits his education in the broad sense of the term. It delays his process of growing up. It needlessly and unnaturally prolongs the period of adolescence. It keeps him from doing what he wants to do and from learning what he wants to learn. It prevents him from acting independently and denies him the chance to assume responsibilities. In the high school he is pressured into meeting the requirements for his diploma, requirements which are admittedly arbitrary. He perceives the diploma as meaningless in and of itself except as a kind of passport to the real world created by adults to keep young people out for as long as possible.

Many high school students, we are told, *feel* cut off because they *are* cut off from the main stream of life, from where the action is. They feel, because they are, useless, unproductive, insignificant, having no real responsibility, making no important contribution to anyone or anything, not even to themselves. Excluded from adult society, they are forced into a subculture of their own where, in order to alleviate their frustrations or simply to overcome their boredom, their main preoccupation becomes a senseless kind of pursuit of fun and kicks.

The romantic reformers whom I have been paraphrasing are not, of course, talking about all youth. For some young people, they would agree, high school and the adolescent experience is really not so bad and most of them turn out pretty well despite their having been kept in custody for four of the best years of their lives. It is no wonder to the romantics that some adolescents feel alienated and are rebellious. What is surprising is that more of them are not.

THE OUTMODED HIGH SCHOOL

The American high school, we are reminded by its critics, is a product of the nineteenth century, designed for a different kind of world from that of today. Until well into the twentieth century, the school was a person's main, if not his only, source of knowledge about history, geography, literature, science, art, mathematics, and other academic subjects. Television, films, radio, tapes and records, inexpensive books and proliferation of magazines, and the ease of travel, among other things, have changed all that. No longer is a person as dependent upon his teachers and textbooks for knowledge as his grandparents were. As a matter of fact, his opportunities for acquiring knowledge quickly, pleasantly, efficiently, dramatically, and inexpensively are far greater than they would have dreamed possible. But the schools continue to function as though they were still the main, if not the only, source of knowledge.

In previous generations, the main source of a person's education was considered to be his home, his family, and his community. Thereby helping his father with the chores, for example, or by helping her mother in the kitchen, the young person learned the kinds of things that really mattered: how to do a useful job, how to relate to others, how to cooperate, how to earn a living, how to take his place in the community, how to be a good father or mother or husband or wife. There he learned, because he was expected to assume, a sense of responsibility for doing something important. Others depended on him. If he didn't bring in the firewood, there would be no firewood and the whole family could freeze to death, or at least have to go without their hot coffee. He felt needed and important because he was. He didn't have to wonder about his identity. He knew.

21

The academic knowledge he learned in high school, if he went, was largely ornamental, relatively unimportant, and certainly not essential. It was nice to have, but one could get along quite well without it. If a person wanted or thought he needed academic knowledge, the school was the place to get it. But the really important things were learned at home. Due to industrialization, urbanization, changing patterns of family life, and a great many other economic and sociological factors, such we are told is no longer the case. The high school is still there to supply the academic knowledge, but homes can no longer be counted on, as they once were, to help the young person grow into adulthood.

Would-be reformers recommend that, since newer and better ways of acquiring knowledge are readily available to those who want to learn, the traditional knowledge-dispensing function of the high school be de-emphasized. They point out that what today's young people want and need are genuine responsibilities and opportunities for productive activity, such as their ancestors had, but that many of them do not have such opportunities in their homes, nor are they getting them anywhere else. They believe, therefore, that the high school should assume a new purpose, the purpose formerly filled in the home, that of developing the young person's abilities to function as a responsible, productive adult.

If the high school is to be thought of as a custodial institution, a means of keeping kids off the street and maybe even entertained for a while, it is indeed something new in the history of education, a kind of institution unheard of and certainly unnecessary until well into the twentieth century. But if that's what a high school is, much less expensive and even more entertaining baby-sitting services could surely be provided.

If, on the other hand, the high school is thought of primarily as a place, maybe the best or even the only place, where an adolescent can learn subject matter, it has perhaps outlived its usefulness. If, however, the high school is thought of as a means of providing for the real needs and overall development of twentieth-going-on-twenty-first century youth, then, the romantic critics maintain, it is sorely in need of a major overhauling.

CONSERVATIVE CRITICS

As we have noted, the romantic critics of education and their counterparts, the humanistic psychologists, hold that the function of our schools should be much broader than that of simply imparting information or developing traditional cognitive skills. But they find many of our schools to be grossly ineffective even with respect to such limited traditional objectives as teaching subject matter and the three R's. This shortcoming, moreover, has been noted and deplored by a host of other critics who by no stretch of the imagination could be regarded as romantics.

Hard-headed legislators, middle-American parents, efficiency-minded businessmen, ivory-tower-type academicians, no-nonsense journalists, and a great many behavioristic psychologists, among others, are tremendously upset by the readily-available statistics showing that many high school graduates are incapable of reading above the fourth or fifth grade level on standardized tests. In the business world, as well as through informal contacts, these anything-but-romantic critics have also found that many possessors of a high school diploma cannot spell or write a complete sentence or even fill out a simple job application form properly; that they cannot solve simple problems in mathematics, have no comprehension of grammar or syntax, know very little about history of geography or science or how the government works; that they know little and care less about literature or economics or current events; that they have no appreciation of music or art; and that they cannot carry on a conversation without using "like" and "yinno" at least three times in each sentence.

These "back to the basics" conservative critics and the romantics disagree on what the nature of the remedy is, and even on the seriousness of the problem. But on this point, unlike the other criticisms we have thus far considered, they are in general agreement that many of our schools are falling short. While the romantics as a group are favorably disposed toward the kinds of recommendations discussed in Chapter 3, the conservative critics would probably feel somewhat more comfortable with the behavioristic system which is summarized in Chapter 5.

FAILURE TO TEACH GOOD CITIZENSHIP

Generally speaking, the conservative critics are not nearly as concerned as the romantics with the alleged neglect of affective education. In fact, they are inclined to argue that the schools have already gone too far in the direction of education for "mental health," and that teachers should concentrate on teaching, instead of dabbling in psychotherapy. But there is one aspect of affective education with which they have been very much concerned. This is the area of what has been called character education or education for good citizenship.

The conservative critics note, as they can hardly help noting, a great deal of bad citizenship in the world: stealing, cheating, lying, stabbing, vandalizing, disregard of authority, disrespect for the rights of others, etc. They note that much of this antisocial behavior is being perpetrated by young people of school age or by those who have recently left school. They conclude that the schools have not been doing a particularly good job of producing good citizens. They maintain that along with "basic" subject matter and intellectual skills, our schools should more effectively teach those moral principles and social standards that adult society expects the younger generation to observe. They readily concede that this type of training is primarily the responsibility of parents, but they believe that the school has an important role to play in this area and has opportunities which it has sadly neglected.

24

The romantics, of course, are also concerned with the problem of education for good citizenship but again they do not agree with the conservatives on the nature of the problem or its remedy. According to the conservative critics, and contrary to what the romantics have been telling us, a big part of the problem is that young people have too much freedom in the schools, that they have in effect been taught they have a right to do just about anything they please and "get away" with it. Although they do not all necessarily recommend a strict, autocratic, law and order approach, they do call for a tightening up of discipline and the restoration of teachers and principals to positions of authority.

IN DEFENSE OF THE SCHOOLS

The criticisms which have just been summarized have not gone unchallenged. There have been no best-selling books blasting the romantic or the conservative critics as they have blasted the educational establishment, nor have defenders of the system been given much, if any, time on TV talk shows to tell what a fine job they think the schools have been doing. But in a substantial number of professional journal articles, in reviews of some of the romantics' books, at various educational conferences and workshops, and perhaps most frequently in teachers' lounges over coffee, counter-critics, spokesmen for the educational establishment, hard-working teachers, and conscientious school administrators have stated their case. Briefly, it is this: Our schools are admittedly not perfect, and neither are the teachers and administrators who staff them, or the board members who manage them. But they are not nearly as bad as the hatchet-men have made them out to be. Every year they turn out thousands upon thousands of young people who are good, literate, decent, well-informed, productive, law-abiding, reasonably happy citizens. The schools must be doing something right.

25

Some of the defects pointed out by the critics are worthy of note, but most of them have been grossly exaggerated and sensationalized. The cases they cite to document their criticisms are isolated incidents which are hardly typical of the educational system as a whole. It is as though they toured the country from coast to coast seeking out the most deplorable situations they could find and tried to pass these off as an accurate picture of what American education is like. The critics, in short, have been guilty of one of the most grievous sins in scholarship: overgeneralizing from a few extreme cases.

The counter-critics assume the validity of the school's traditional objectives as I believe the majority of students and their parents do. What is needed, they claim, is not a new set of goals, but more effective means of attaining such traditional goals as the imparting of knowledge, the cultivation of intellectual skills, the development of moral values, and the formation of good citizens. Among the needed means are such things as smaller classes, more equipment, better facilities, more instructional aids—things, in short, which money can buy. But as urgent as financial support is, the moral support and confidence and cooperation of parents and the public at large is equally necessary if the school is to succeed.

Defenders of the existing educational system are quick to point out that some of the most vocal of the critics have had little or no concentrated elementary or high school teaching experience. Never having been on the firing line, or finding themselves unable to stand the heat and fleeing from the classroom to the more lucrative occupation of defaming teachers, these critics don't know the facts of life. Realistically, the counter-critics claim, the detractors should recognize that the school cannot work miracles, that it cannot solve all the world's problems, that it cannot fully compensate for a child's bad home life or unhappy family situation or for a poor environment or for poor genes. So, under the circumstances and all things considered, the job that our schools have been doing has been by no means all that bad. In fact, they insist, it's been pretty damned good.

Like the TV talk shows and the newspapers, I haven't given the counter-critics nearly as much time or space as I have to the critics. Neither have I given the conservative critics as much attention as the romantics received. But I think that enough has been said to give you the flavor of the conservatives' and counter-critics' points of view Besides, the anti-romantics have their innings coming up in Chapters 4 and 5.

LOOKING AHEAD

Whether or not the counter-critics are right, or whether or to what extent any or all of the romantic or conservative criticisms are valid, is a matter that I certainly wish you would think about and try to decide for yourself. Some of the criticisms, you will have noted, are (or at least seem to be) in direct contradiction to one another: the conservative arguing, for example, that today's students have "too much" freedom and the romantics insisting that they do not have nearly enough; or the romantics claiming that the schools have overemphasized cognitive objectives to the neglect of students' personality development, while the conservatives find that just the opposite has been done. The teacher, then, finds herself in a "damned if she does and damned if she doesn't" situation. No matter what she does, she can be pretty sure that someone will find fault.

Fault-finding is certainly not the purpose of this book, nor is it a defense of the established ways of doing things. I have not devoted the biggest part of this chapter to criticisms for negative, destructive purposes. I have presented them as a point of departure for the discussion which will follow in the remaining chapters, as a kind of background for a better understanding of the improvements (or alleged or expected improvements) in the educational system that are being tried, or at least recommended, by two groups of educational psychologists: humanists and behaviorists.

Practically every classroom practice or procedure, practially every method of teaching and plan for curriculum organization, practically every innovation and recommendation can be traced back to or is related to either humanistic or behavioral psychology or some combination of the two. Having examined some of the more common romantic criticisms, which have been derived from humanistic psychology, we shall in the next chapter consider some of the basic principles and philosophical assumptions of humanism. Chapter 3 will deal in a far more positive way than this chapter with the kinds of practices the humanists recommend.

2

Humanism
*You Know,
Doing Your Own Thing*

Prior to about the middle of the twentieth century, the two dominant psychological systems, not only in America but throughout the world, were Freudian psychology (or psychoanalysis) and behaviorism (or S-R, for stimulus-response, psychology.) Humanism was developed and began to emerge in the late 1940s at least in part as a reaction to, or outgrowth of, those two systems. For that reason, it is commonly referred to as the *third force* in psychology.

Of the two earlier systems, behaviorism has had and continues to have a greater and more direct effect on educational psychology and the work of the schools. Since Freud's greatest contributions were in the area of clinical psychology, the effects of his theories on formal education have been, for the most part, indirect. With respect to the schools, his influence has been more pronounced in the affective than the cognitive domain. He offered no theory of learning, no practical advice on the methodology of teaching. But his ideas have been applied to such areas as discipline, character development and, of course, the student's mental health. The principles of behaviorism have also been applied to these problems. Besides, behaviorism does offer a theory of learning and a great deal of practical advice on how to teach.

Those who eventually came to be called humanistic psychologists readily concede that Freudian and behavioral psychology have contributed significantly to our understanding of the dynamics of human conduct. They recognize that Freud opened up a whole new world for psychology: the world of the unconscious. The traditional pre-Freudian view of human behavior was that a person's acts are rational and deliberate.

Man was presumed to know not only what he was doing but why he was doing it, and it was believed that he freely chose to act that way. Freud challenged these notions. He claimed that much human behavior is irrational, that it is determined by repressed unconscious drives, by man's instinctive tendencies toward sexual satisfaction and violence or destruction, and that a person's motives, as well as the real meaning of his acts, are often unknown to the person himself.

Humanists do not deprecate some of the basic Freudian insights about the human personality and its operations, nor do they minimize the role that psychoanalysis has played in helping us arrive at a deeper understanding of those who are neurotic or emotionally disturbed. But they find that Freudian psychology leaves a great deal to be desired as an adequate explanation of much ordinary everyday behavior on the part of "normal" people.

Humanists also respect the contributions of the early behaviorists and their efforts to make psychology an exact science based on empirical data, experimentation, and the rigid methodological principles of physics, chemistry, and zoology, but they believe that, as valuable as behaviorism has been in helping us understand some of the simple animal-like behaviors of man, it is too mechanistic, too deterministic, too dehumanizing, and far from acceptable as an explanation of man's higher and distinctively human behavior.

In short, humanists believe that neither Freud nor the behaviorists come to grips with such matters as human goals, purposes, and values; with man's consciousness or awareness, his individuality, personal responsibility or striving for fulfillment; with love, creativity, transcendental experiences or man's inclination toward the mystical. Above all, they feel that neither of the two older psychological systems deals satisfactorily with the matter of human freedom.

Among those who contributed significantly to the development of third force psychology are Abraham Maslow, Carl Rogers, Rollo May, Erich Fromm, Gordon Allport, Prescott Lecky, Arthur Combs, and a number of other individuals who have also been classified as existentialists or phenomenologists or perceptualists or personalists. The third force, then, is a kind of loosely-organized coalition. Its members differ among themselves on a number of particulars, but they are in general agreement enough on basic principles and assumptions to warrant their being grouped together.

THE HUMAN PERSON

Among the common principles that unite the humanists are their assumptions about the human personality. They believe that a person is much more than an elaborate, sophisticated machine. They believe that he is essentially different from subhuman forms of life, that he cannot be fully understood much less appreciated by sole reliance on laboratory-type scientific research, and that he cannot be adequately described in terms of statistics, graphs, and charts. Instead of the objective, analytic, detached, external approach to the study of man favored by their behavioral counterparts, humanists use a more personal, subjective, introspective, phenomenological approach, or what they call an internal frame of reference.

Humanists are not as much concerned with a person's observable, measurable behavior as they are with his feelings, attitudes, beliefs, purposes, and values—with those "inner behaviors" that make an individual person distinctively and uniquely human. To understand another person, they maintain, it is necessary to "get into his skin," to see the world and the individual himself, not as they exist in "objective reality" but as they appear to him here and now. This concern with the person's internal life, with his experiences as he interprets them, and with what he thinks or feels or believes about himself and other people, is basic to humanistic psychology and is discussed at somewhat greater length later in this chapter.

Humanists also posit the natural goodness of man and his tremendous potential for growth. They believe that every person has intrinsic value and dignity simply because he is a living human being. Some of them maintain that man is at least figuratively, if not literally, made in the "image and likeness of God" or that there is something sacred (or almost sacred) about everyone. In this regard they are fond of quoting Shakespeare:

> What a piece of work is man! how noble in reason! how infinite in faculty! in form and moving how express and admirable! in action how like an angel! in apprehension how like a god!

Or the Bible:

> What is man that thou art mindful of him? and the son of man, that thou visitest him? For thou hast made him a little lower than the angels, and has crowned him with glory and honour.

They believe, therefore, that every individual is deserving of the highest respect. They believe that every person is unique, and that this uniqueness should also be respected and cultivated, rather than repressed or levelled off.

They believe that humans are by nature social beings and that some form of democracy, implying equality, is the best means of social organization in the home and school as well as in one's country and community. They believe that every person, not just adults, has an "inalienable right to life, liberty and the pursuit of happiness." They believe that every individual needs help in reaching the happiness he is entitled to and in developing or actualizing his particular set of potentialities. They believe that "formal" education in the school as well as "informal" education in the home should be primarily concerned with providing that kind of help.

FREEDOM

Central to the thinking of most humanists is the concept of personal autonomy, the individual's capacity for self-determination, or what is commonly referred to as free will. They believe that the freedom to choose is one of the most distinctively human characteristics and very likely the most important. According to the humanists, a person's behavior is not determined by mysterious repressed urges or traumatic childhood experiences which lie buried in the deep recesses of the unconscious mind. Nor is it determined by powerful external forces over which the individual has no control and which he might not even be aware of. Human behavior is, rather, largely a consequence of one's own choices.

One's heredity and environment certainly affect his behavior, according to the humanists, but they do not determine it. They believe that man has to a very high degree, though not perfectly or completely, the capacity to choose how he will act within the limitations that may have been imposed on him by his heredity. He cannot, of course, decide some day that he's going to be tall enough to play center on a professional basketball team when his genes have determined that his mature height will be somewhere around 5 feet 6 inches. But all sorts of choices are open to him as to the kind of 5½ footer he is going to be. He is, moreover, free to decide how he will react to the environmental stimuli he encounters. Perhaps he cannot single-handedly or overnight change the neighborhood in which he lives or his socioeconomic status. But again all sorts of choices are open to him as to how he will live within that environment. Contrary to the admitted determinism of the Freudians and many of the behaviorists, humanists maintain, in short, that every person is free to set his own goals and to select the means he will employ to attain them.

Man's capacity for self-determination underlies his capacity for self-regulation, self-assertion, and self-actualization. It is implicit in such concepts as personal integrity and responsibility, initiative and creativity, altruism and love, and in the very notions of justice, morality, and citizenship. For these reasons, humanistic psychology is very much concerned with the preservation and cultivation of individual freedom, and is often thought to be especially appropriate for a democratic society.

NATURAL GOODNESS

Another basic assumption of the humanists has to do with their view of human nature. At the risk of oversimplification, one could say that human nature according to Freud is essentially bad, according to the behaviorists it is neutral, and according to the humanists it is fundamentally good.

In Freudian psychology, the core of the human personality, the very essence of human nature out of which everything else including the ego and superego develops, is the id. Id, you may recall, is the name Freud gave to what he regarded as man's universal instinctive tendencies toward sexual gratification, often in a perverted form, and toward violence, aggression, destruction, and death. Impulses arising from the id and demands for gratification of these impulses can be controlled by the ego (the rational part of man) and the superego (essentially the internalized teachings of one's parents), but the id itself cannot be changed. The id is what a person basically is—amoral, impulsive, governed solely by the pleasure principle, demanding immediate satisfaction with no concern whatsoever for the consequences or for other people. Not a very pretty portrayal of human nature, but according to the Freudians an accurate, realistic view.

According to behaviorism, human nature is neither good nor bad because there is no such thing as human nature and it is kind of ridiculous to even talk about it. Everything a person does, including his so-called inclinations, tendencies, and predispositions, is a learned response. So are a person's goals, standards, values, beliefs, and you name it. It is fruitless, therefore, and potentially dangerous to look for the sources of man's behavior in his so-called nature. A person is not born good or naturally bad; he acquires good or bad ways of acting. This matter will be dealt with at greater length in Chapter 4.

Very much in the philosophical tradition of Jean Jacques Rousseau, who would certainly have to be numbered among their intellectual forebearers, humanists are inclined to the position that man is naturally, inherently, good, that is, trustworthy, friendly, dependable, well-intentioned, predisposed to be helpful, capable of choosing wisely and of regulating his own life. In fact, man is not only capable of, but is striving toward, a kind of moral perfection. If he has the necessary freedom and encouragement and support, he can and inevitably will develop in a manner that will be beneficial to himself as an individual and to other people and society at large as well.

This view of human nature strains the credulity of many people and impresses them as hopelessly naive. They look for supporting evidence but have a hard time finding any. Evidence for the opposite point of view or for the behavioristic position seems to be much more plentiful. Perhaps you now see more clearly why the humanists are referred to as romantics. But the humanists are dead serious in maintaining that the fewer restrictions or controls over another person's behavior, the better it will be for all concerned. Unsocial or antisocial and immoral behavior can almost always be traced back to misguided intervention in the other person's affairs or frustrations of his normal developmental patterns. Without such interference, development naturally tends toward the social and moral as man's innate goodness has a chance to manifest itself.

GROWTH AND HUMAN POTENTIAL

The concept of man's moral perfectability and his natural tendencies toward socialization is part of a broader assumption that is basic to the humanistic position. This assumption has to do with man's tremendous potential and his striving to fulfill it. According to the humanists, one of the key principles of psychology is that people are constantly growing—not only and not primarily in a physical manner, but in a much more comprehensive way as they seek to expand and enhance their total being. This accounts for another cardinal characteristic of human nature, man's unceasing restlessness.

Humanists are well aware of limits to human development imposed on individuals by their heredity and environment. But these limitations are nowhere near as restrictive as they are sometimes thought to be. No one ever realizes his full potential; in fact, we are just beginning to discover how great the human potential really is. Without suggesting that Jonathan Livingston Human has the potential to fly with his own power higher and faster than any bird has ever flown or that he can transcend time and space through sheer determination, the humanists not only recognize and emphasize man's longing to be somehow better than he presently is, but also offer abundant encouragement that he indeed can become a fuller, more perfect human being.

GOALS

Humanistic psychologists, as we have seen, recognize the effects of heredity and environment on a person's behavior. They recognize the existence of repressed wishes and unconscious drives. They concede that some forms of behavior are attributable to the individual's previous conditioning. But none of these determine his behavior. Of far greater moment are the means he chooses to attain his goals.

Neither Freudians nor behaviorists are much concerned with a person's goals per se. In humanistic psychology they are essential to an understanding of his behavior. To explain human behavior, Freudians and behaviorists alike are inclined to look toward the individual's past, toward his early childhood experiences or his previous conditioning, to try to find the relevant historical antecedents of the particular behavior in question.

The assumption that an individual is pretty much bound by his past along with the fact that the past cannot be changed accounts for the strong element of determinism, and a certain pessimism, in these two systems.

Humanistic psychology is not so much concerned with the individual's past experiences as it is with his present purposes or intentions. Unlike historical causes, one's intentions can be revised as his perceptions are revised and as he accumulates new experiences. Goals, moreover, always pertain to the present in relation to the future. Thus, humanism is sometimes regarded as more forward-looking and optimistic than the other two systems. Still, as we shall see in Chapter 4, behaviorists as a group might be considered just as optimistic as humanists, and maybe even more so.

One of the key assumptions of third force psychology is that man is a purposeful, goal-seeking organism. Just about everything he does is done in order to satisfy some need or attain some goal. In order to understand what a person is doing and why he is doing it, it is therefore necessary to understand what his goals are.

Every person's immediate goals may differ from everyone else's in particular detail, and they might change from day to day or even more frequently than that. But all people have certain general goals in common simply because they are human beings. These goals do not change, nor are they ever completely attained. Most of these goals correspond to the satisfaction of one's need for self-preservation and self-enhancement.

Self-preservation may be the most basic of all human needs. But self-preservation involves more for a human being than the maintenance of life or simple survival. Man has the need to preserve his psychological (or phenomenological) as well as his physical self. Thus, in addition to wanting and needing food, shelter, and other things that pertain to his physical security and comfort, he also wants and needs acceptance, affection, a feeling of affiliation, freedom from fear and threat, and other gratifiers which contribute to his emotional security or to the preservation of his psychological self.

But mere preservation of self, physically and psychologically, is not enough. Man also wants and needs to grow, to develop, to expand himself, to feel adequate in situations that he regards as important, to be looked up to, respected and admired by others, and maybe even envied a bit—but at the very least to be noticed. The purpose of much human behavior is to satisfy one or some combination of these kinds of needs.

THE SELF

Humanists are very much interested in the *self*. In fact, their system of psychology is sometimes referred to as the self-theory. Their literature abounds with references to such ideas as self-actualization, self-consistency, self-awareness, self-enhancement, self-acceptance, self-esteem, self-image, self-confidence, and self-concept, as well as the phenomenological self, the congruent self, the authentic self, and the fully-functioning self. This emphasis on the self does not, of course, imply selfishness or self-centeredness in the sense of exclusive preoccupation with one's own welfare without regard for the best interests of others. It does, however, imply that one's self is at the very heart of his own private universe, the most vital part of the world as he knows it, the object of his deepest concern.

The self is so tremendously complex yet so utterly simple that it does not lend itself to easy definition. Trying to explain in words what the self is is something like trying to define the personal pronouns I or me. As the term self is commonly used by humanists it refers to the sum total of everything that you, for example, regard as distinctively yours: your body, your memories, your attitudes, your potentialities, your aspirations, feelings, experiences, and values—whatever, in short, it is that distinguishes you from anyone else. In a way, even your friends and relatives, your personal possessions and other physical objects are among the components of your self. When a person states, for example, that Paris or basketball or Shakespeare or his wife "will always be a part of me," humanists understand what he means.

The self, however, is not a mere collection of parts. It is the synthesis, the organization, the interrelations of all of the traits, qualities, characteristics, and experiences that go to make up an individual human being—the binding spirit, as it were, that holds them all together and gives them meaning. This is why the humanists insist that education must be concerned with the whole child, not simply with his cognitive development, but with his physical, social, emotional, aesthetic, moral, attitudinal, and psychosexual development as well.

According to the humanists, the individual self is, or should be, the alpha and the omega of the educational and developmental process. Since a person has only one life to live and one self to develop, his self is something that he must learn to cherish and cultivate. He, as well as those who have the responsibility for guiding his development, must realize that whoever he is, he is something special. He is someone who has never existed before and will never exist again. His purpose in life, as well as his greatest need, is to become to the fullest extent possible what he and he alone is capable of becoming, and to do what he and he alone is capable of doing.

SELF-ACTUALIZATION

Man's loftiest and most distinctively human goal, according to third force psychology, is self-actualization, also referred to as self-fulfillment or self-realization. Man's other goals reflect some particular deficiency to be filled or some need to be met, such as the need for food or recognition. Not so with self-actualization. Self-actualization presumes that those kinds of needs have already been met. In fact, the satisfaction of one's needs for self-preservation and self-enhancement can be thought of as prerequisites for self-actualization. When and only when a person is reasonably well satisfied with respect to his physical and safety needs and his needs for love and esteem does self-actualization emerge as a goal. Then and only then is the individual capable of actualizing himself. Having satisfied his "lower order" needs, he now strives for the development of his individuality, the expression of his uniqueness, the realization of potentialities. He strives, in other words, to become fully himself, which is to say a self-actualizing person.

A self-actualizing individual is a real, genuine, authentic person, not a shadow of someone else. He is a one-of-a-kind original, not a reproduction. He is inner rather than outer directed. He is morally and intellectually free. He lives his life in what for him is the richest, happiest, most productive and satisfying way possible. Having satisfied his needs for acceptance and approval, he does not have to bother with trying to impress others or win their esteem. His energies, rather, are directed toward personal growth, toward the realization of his unique set of potentialities.

As we have noted, third force psychologists believe that human potentialities are usually not fully realized and that man rarely becomes what he is capable of becoming. The reason for this is that for some people life is literally a struggle for survival, for psychological if not physical self-preservation. These people (and here, I think, the humanists would include the vast majority) are so preoccupied with their needs for security and love and esteem and recognition, and expend so much of their energies attempting to satisfy them that they never quite get around to being themselves, do not realize what they are missing, and never even think about the matter very much.

Every person, according to humanists, whether he is consciously aware of the fact or not, wants to "make something" of himself. What he wants to make and how he makes it is necessarily an individual matter. Similarly, every person wants to get something out of life and to leave his mark. Every person wants happiness. But precisely what he wants from life and what happiness means to him are also individual matters. Thus, while every person is striving for self-fulfillment, every person has (or is) a unique self to fulfill. Depending upon a complex of variable and circumstances, an individual might fulfill himself, or try to, as an artist, an athlete, a parent, a teacher, a scientist, as a man or woman, as a Christian or a Jew, as an Irishman or an American. He might acheive a measure of self-actualization by cooking a meal, selling shoes, looking at the stars, driving a taxicab, by writing a book or by reading a book, and in a countless variety of other ways that he might find personally rewarding and that he feels contribute to making himself a fuller human being. Self-actualization, then, is not so much a matter of what a person does, as how he feels about what he's doing.

PERCEPTION

Another basic principle of humanistic psychology has to do with perception. Humanists maintain that the manner in which a person responds to stimuli which he encounters depends upon how he perceives those stimuli, and how he perceives himself, his fellow man, and the world that he feels he is a part of. Perception is a key process in all human behavior, including the selection of one's goals and the means of attaining them.

Perception is the process by which an individual interprets or derives meaning from his experience. It pertains to what a person "sees" in a situation and what he does as a consequence. What I do in a given situation, according to this point of view, depends not so much on what's "out there" in objective reality, but what's in my so-called mind's eye. This is the thing, of course, about beauty being in the eye of the beholder.

Perception is always selective and personal. Consider, for example, the cluster of images evoked by the word Christmas. Whatever the dictionary definition of that word might be, it certainly does not "mean" the same thing to a devout Christian as it does to a non-Christian, or to a child as it does to his parents. Merchants, postal workers, lonely senior citizens, rich people, poor people, bachelors, married men with families all have different perceptions of what Christmas "is." Each person's perceptions are highly individual, depending as they do on his own background of previous experience, his level of maturity, his particular goals, and the surrounding circumstances that constitute his personal frame of reference.

In order to understand another person's behavior, it is necessary to enter into his world, to step into his shoes, see the world as it seems to him, and try to feel things as he feels them. Because man himself is constantly changing and his environment is constantly changing, his perceptions are constantly changing. Thus, the high element of relativism in this perceptual or phenomenological position. What is perceived as true or good or beautiful or appropriate or necessary or bad by one person is not always or necessarily perceived in the same way by another person, or for that matter by the same person in different circumstances. But however an individual perceives a situation at a given moment constitutes reality for that person at that particular time.

The only reality a humanist is likely to be concerned with is what has been termed personal or psychological reality, that is, the meaning that a person's environment has for him here and now. If an object or a situation has no actual or potential meaning to an individual, if it has no relevance that he can see to his life, it might just as well not exist as far as he is concerned. In fact, for him, in a very real sense, it does not exist. Things have no inherent, absolute meanings in and of themselves. They derive their meaning from their relationship to other things and to the individual perceiver. The full implications of this principle for education, which is supposed to be meaningful, are just beginning to be realized.

The importance of perception in humanistic psychology and the high degree of subjectivity in the perceptual process would be difficult to exaggerate. A person's attitudes, feelings, beliefs and values, as well as his outward, more readily observable behavior, are all consequences of his personal perceptions. Of all human perceptions, there is none more vital in third force psychology than the individual's perceptions of himself and his resultant self-concept.

SELF-CONCEPT

Every person, according to the humanists, lives in two worlds: the public world of objective reality and in his own private world. This private world is what we have referred to as one's personal or psychological environment. It has also been called one's life space or phenomenological field. By whatever name it is called, at the very center of this private universe is the individual self. Corresponding to these two worlds are two dimensions of this self: what one "really" is and what he thinks or feels he is. The latter, his self-concept, is his personal, subjective impression of who he is. It includes his feelings about, attitudes toward, and evaluation of himself, and his ideas of how he fits into the scheme of things.

A person's self-concept is both a cause of his present behavior and an effect of his past experiences. It is an effect in that one's feelings about himself depend to a great extent on his previous record of successes and failures, on the quality of his interactions with other people, and on what he thinks other people think of him. It is a cause in that his self-concept may have a greater bearing on what he does or how he does it than his objective status. A child who feels that he is too dumb to learn how to read will in all probability have a difficult time with reading even though his readiness test scores are quite high. One who has been told repeatedly that he is bad can be expected to begin, or continue, acting in a bad manner.

From the mental health standpoint, the person who considers himself intelligent, capable, good looking, and popular, even though by any available objective standards he is dull, inept, ugly, and rejected, has a certain advantage over his counterpart who objectively has these desirable features but feels that he lacks them. Similarly, whether or not a person actually *is* loved might not be as crucial for his personality adjustment as whether he *feels* loved. In the areas of counseling and psychotherapy, humanistic psychologists regard the individual's self-concept as the number one consideration, maintaining that a person's behavior cannot be changed or his symptoms of maladjustment alleviated without a prior change in his feelings about himself.

As we noted in the first chapter, humanistically-inclined educators believe that schools ought to be a lot more concerned than they are with helping students develop favorable self-concepts. In fact, I do not know of any educational goal to which they would assign a higher priority.

Dewey

SOCIAL RELATIONS

Despite their strong and apparently endless emphasis on individuality, self-enhancement, self-actualization, self-concept and the like, our humanistic friends are equally concerned with the person's social relationships. They make much of the fact that man is by nature a social being, dependent upon others not only for his survival, but also for the satisfaction of his needs for love and recognition, affiliation and esteem. They also stress the individual's need for involvement with others in order to develop his potential because there is only one way he can fulfill himself, and that is in some particular society.

The emphasis on the self, therefore, carries with it no implications of selfishness as that term is ordinariliy used, or of any unhealthy, unsocial kind of self-centeredness. Quite the contrary. The fully-functioning, self-actualizing person, whom the humanists hold up as an ideal, experiences a deep feeling of identification with others, has strong feelings of sympathy with and affection for them, and a genuine desire to help them. He perceives his interests as being not in conflict but in harmony with those of his fellow man.

The optimistic view of human nature held by third forcers includes the assumption that man is naturally inclined toward such virtues as generosity, cooperation, and altruism. As the individual is personally fulfilled, his concept of his self is expanded so as to embrace his family, his associates, his community, and eventually perhaps all members of the human race. He comes to perceive himself as part of them, and them, in a very real sense, as part of himself.

Historically, one of the first areas of humanistic psychology to develop and gain widespread acceptance was group dynamics, the branch of social psychology that is concerned with the structure and function of groups of people and their effects on individual behavior. A key assumption of group dynamics is that an individual's behavior cannot be understood apart from the social context in which it takes place. In other words, the group of which a person happens to be a part at a given moment often has a decisive effect on his behavior. Most of us do not behave at funerals in quite the same way we act at weddings. We might not act at a public meeting precisely as we would in the privacy of our own homes with a few old friends—or for that matter with one friend as we might with another.

The sensitivity training movement of the 1960s emerged as an outgrowth of group dynamics. This movement has taken a variety of forms in an attempt to improve human relations by bringing about a deeper awareness of one's own feelings as well as those of others. The very term sensitivity, as well as such concepts as awareness, encounter, dialogue, social consciousness, concern, empathy, commitment, and meaningful relationship, terms which have become household expressions, owe their popularity, if not their origins, to humanistic psychology. These concepts suggest that third force psychologists hardly regard man as an island, selfishly seeking nothing but his own fulfillment, but rather as a person who wants and needs other people.

HUMANISM AND PROTEST

Third force psychology began to emerge in the 1940s, was developed in the 1950s, and spread most rapidly in the 1960s.

As we have seen, it arose as a reaction (really a protest) against what were perceived as the deterministic, mechanistic, dehumanizing features of older psychological systems. It is more than coincidental that this new force gained such wide acceptance and came to enjoy such broad popularity at the time it did, in that decade of protest, the 1960s.

Humanistic psychology has had an especially strong appeal to social activists and reformers, political liberals, members of the radical left, and the highly idealist; to those who were oppressed or felt they were oppressed or sympathized with others who were oppressed; to those who were for any reason disillusioned or dissatisfied with the status quo; to those who felt they were unduly restrained by their parents, their teachers, their government, their church, their employers, or by social conventions, traditions, laws, or the so-called establishment. These and others who were hip, or thought they were or tried to convey the impression that they were, were attracted by the humanists' emphasis on freedom, individuality, self-expression, love, the human potential, and above all self-actualization, which was translated into the vernacular of the period as: Man, like, you know, I mean, doing your own thing.

Being itself a kind of protest movement, humanistic psychology tied in nicely with various other protest movements in the 1960s. It lent support to the civil rights movement, the women's liberation and student liberation and gay liberation movements, to the anti-war and anti-police and anti-authority and anti-school movements, and to just about any cause that promised liberation from just about anything, or that exalted freedom in any area from clothing and hair styles to abortion and alternatives to marriage.

As the principles and particularly the slogans of humanistic psychology became popularized, all sorts of people from all walks of life began applying them to themselves. Factory employees, for example, discovered that their monotonous work was dehumanizing. Their wives discovered that housework did not begin to tap their potentialities. College students discovered that their courses were irrelevant. Businessmen discovered that they were not fulfilling themselves as human beings. Clergymen discovered that traditional religions were not meaningful. Members of the armed forces discovered that their freedom and individuality were being violated. Prisoners discovered that their human dignity was being debased. And educational reformers found that all of these discoveries applied in a special way to the schools.

VARIETIES OF HUMANISM

Throughout this chapter I have been generalizing about the beliefs, convictions, and assumptions of a number of individuals to whom I have referred as third force or humanistic psychologists. I have not discussed the differences in the viewpoints of, say, Carl Rogers and Adrian Van Kaam, or Abraham Maslow and Arthur Combs, or the fine points that distinguish an existentialist from a perceptualist, or the particular contributions of such recognized leaders of the movement as Viktor Frankl or Sidney Jourard or James Bugental. It should be understood, therefore, that the principles and assumptions which have just been summarized do not completely or exactly reflect the thinking of any one individual humanist or of any identifiable subgroup of humanists.

Humanists almost have to be highly individualistic. This is why humanistic psychology has taken many different forms with many different points of emphasis. Consider, for example, humanistic positions (note the plural) with respect to religion. In some usages, a humanist by definition is one who disavows anything but the human or the natural. This is true of some humanists, but certainly not all. Since the Renaissance there have been Christian humanists, so called because they integrated the teachings of Jesus and their theological convictions with the classical concept of "the proper study of mankind." Within the Christian framework there are some very conservative, classically-oriented individuals who regard themselves as humanists, as well as Jesus people (to say nothing of Jesus freaks) who also consider themselves Christian humanists. A number of Jews have turned from conservatism or orthodoxy to some form of Jewish humanism. There are Buddhists, Muslims, Hindus, and members of just about every other religious sect in the humanistic camp, and there is still room for atheists, agnostics, and anyone else who wants in.

In order to find themselves, or to fulfill or express themselves, or to discover the meaning of their existence, or to achieve a higher level of consciousness, or to experience a mystical feeling, some self-styled humanists have gotten into yoga or the occult or astrology or drugs or Zen or witchcraft or ESP or transcendental meditation as substitutes for, or supplements to, more traditional systems of religion. So there are a multitude of different positions regarding the transcendental or the mystical that a humanist might take and still be considered a humanist.

Another difference among third force psychologists has to do with their relationships toward other systems of psychology. I have never heard of any reputable psychologist who rejected Freud completely, or who maintained that behaviorists are 100 percent wrong, or that humanists have all of the answers. Every psychologist is indebted to both Freudians and behaviorists and has incorporated, in varying amounts, some of their views into his own system. If the matter could be quantified it might be demonstrated, for example, that a particular psychologist or student of psychology is, say, 60 percent humanist, 25 percent behaviorist, 10 percent Freudian, and 5 percent "other." But even such percentages would fail to tell the whole story since Freudians and neo-Freudians and behaviorists and neo-behaviorists differ among themselves just as humanists do.

Among the common elements that tie the various kinds of so-called humanists together are their assumptions that man is essentially different from subhuman forms of animal life, that he cannot be fully understood through scientific research alone, nor can he be adequately described in terms of statistics, that he is a unique, purposeful, social, essentially good organism with the capacity for self-determination as a means toward self-actualization. Next, let's see what all of this has to do with education.

3

Humanism and Education

*Do We Have To Do
What We Want
To Do?*

Historically the purpose of education has been to transmit something called the cultural heritage. This heritage consisted of knowledge, skills, values, beliefs, customs, myths, etc., which had been handed down in a particular society, pretty much intact, from previous generations. Children were expected to assimilate this culture or way of life because their success, if not their survival, in that society depended on their doing so. What is more, the preservation of that society depended on their doing so.

In primitive societies, with simple cultures, children learned all they needed to know informally, by observation, experience, example, and word of mouth instruction, usually by their parents. As societies grew larger and their cultures too complex to be transmitted informally, the need for teachers and books and schools gradually arose, and education became more formalized. But its purpose remained, and perhaps still is, what it had always been. Only such details as the particular content and methodology have changed. But even in this respect, critics of contemporary education claim that over the past hundred years or so, they really haven't changed all that much.

The concept of education as transmission of the heritage is based on a number of assumptions. One is that older people in positions of authority know for sure what younger people ought to learn. Another is that the next generation will live very much like previous generations and that it will need essentially the same knowledge and skills that had been taught in the past. Still another is that knowledge is static, stable, unchangeable, and that it can be prepackaged into neat little bundles of subject matter which can then be dispensed uniformly and on schedule. Yet another is that the heritage of the past is, if not exactly sacred, certainly worth attempting to perpetuate, even if need be at the expense of more contemporary knowledge and values. Finally, this concept of education seems to imply the necessity of all students learning much the same material as a means of promoting common bonds among them.

Humanistic educators have nothing that I know of against the cultural heritage as such. But they are inclined to challenge these assumptions. As they see it, the purpose of education is considerably broader than passing on the accumulated wisdom and experience of the past. Its purpose, rather, is to help each student learn to be himself, to relate to others, and to live happily here and now as well as to prepare him for a future social role. It is to help him learn how to learn, and to enjoy learning, and to want to continue learning. It is to help him learn to think for himself, to make his own decisions, to formulate his own systems of values and beliefs. It is to help him learn to accept and respect himself and others. It is to help him learn to assume and carry out responsibilities, including the responsibility for his own education. It is to help him learn to love and feel and create and express himself. It is to help him develop whatever talents he might have and to compensate for whatever limitations he might have. The purpose of education, in short, is to help the individual student become a fully-functioning human being. Its focus, therefore, according to the humanists, should not be on the heritage or the material to be learned, but on the student himself.

STUDENT-CENTERED EDUCATION

As an improvement over the conventional teacher-centered classrooms, humanists prefer learning situations that are considerably more student oriented. Their reasoning is that since schools exist primarily for the education of individual students, the instructional process should be based on and geared to their existing interests, problems, and needs. In the conventional classroom, the teacher decides in advance what the students are to learn; she plans, organizes, and directs their work so that they will learn it, and tests them to find out whether or to what extent they have done so. The students' interests and short-range goals might be completely ignored. If they are taken into account at all, they are likely to be used only as means of getting the student to learn what the teacher wants him to learn. She might, for example, capitalize on his interest in batting averages as a means of teaching him how to compute percentages. But his interest in baseball is purely instrumental and incidental. The important thing is teaching him how to compute percentages.

A variety of techniques have been employed in teacher-centered classrooms as steps toward the individualization of instruction or at least as means of providing for individual differences: dividing the class into subgroups, as for reading; the assignment of individual reports or small group projects; the use of programmed textbooks or teaching machines or individually prescribed instructional packets or individualized student-teacher contracts and independent study programs of one kind of another. But humanists contend that all of these, as they are commonly used, are simply devices for getting students to achieve objectives which have been predetermined by teachers or school administrators. They are ways and means of helping the student learn in his own way and at his own rate the material that has been prescribed for him. The romantics like the part about "his own way and at his own rate," but the part about prescribed material is something else.

Allowances are likely to be made for intellectual and other differences among students in a teacher-centered classroom by expecting some of them to learn more or different kinds of things than others. And students might have opportunities to pursue their own interests, if the teacher decides that they are closely enough related to what she wants them to learn. In fact, after the serious learning has been taken care of, if time permits and if the students have behaved themselves, they might be

54

permitted to do, within limits, of course, whatever they want to do. But the decisions are made by the teacher—possibly, but not necessarily, in consultation with the students.

In the opinion of many humanistic educators, concessions to individuality such as these are OK as far as they go, but they really don't go very far. They favor a more fully student-centered concept of education in which the interests and needs, problems and goals, of individuals are not only "taken into account" and used as means, but are the starting point and guiding principles of the entire educational process.

As opposed to the "teacher knows best" philosophy of the conventional school, many of our humanistic friends are convinced that even a very young child, to say nothing of an adolescent, knows better than anyone else what he is ready to learn or needs to learn or should try to learn at any given moment. They believe that instead of trying to meet arbitrary standards and predetermined objectives formulated by someone else, each student should have the freedom and opportunity to concentrate on learning what he wants to learn or feels that he is ready to attempt. They recognize that students at all levels need and should receive guidance, direction, suggestions, and help, but these should be held to a minimum. The emphasis should be not on teaching but on learning, not on what the teacher does but on what the student does. The type of student-centered education recommended by these humanists implies more than a collection of administrative devices or pedagogical gimmicks or half-hearted attempts at individualization. Rather, it involves an all-out commitment to the concept that every student be free to learn what he wants to, when he wants to, because he wants to.

SUMMERHILL

A classic example of the kind of school favored by the romantics is Summerhill. Summerhill is a private coeducational boarding school located about a hundred miles or so from London. It was founded in the early 1920s by A. S. Neill and his wife. Their basic idea was to make the school fit the child instead of the traditional vice versa. Summerhill began as an experimental school but is now more of a demonstration school, attracting visitors from all over the world who have been flocking there to see, not whether, but how, freedom in education works.

Freedom is the guiding principle of Summerhill. Neill, who died in 1973, had an abiding faith in the natural goodness and inherent wisdom of children. He felt that the main goal of life is happiness, so happiness is the main goal of his school. No child at Summerhill is ever required to do anything he doesn't want to do. He is, on the contrary, allowed to do just about anything he pleases with the only stipulation being that he doesn't infringe on the rights of others. This is not to say that there are no rules at Summerhill. In fact, there are many rules, but they are all formulated by the students themselves at their weekly meetings where each student and member of the faculty has one vote.

Class attendance is strictly optional. There is no attendance-taking, no academic requirements, no examinations, no grades. There are schedules, but these apply only to the teachers. They are expected to be in specified places at specified times to teach the usual subjects or skills that would be taught in any English school. If students wish to avail themselves of these opportunities, fine. If not, that's their business. Students have been known to absent themselves from classes for a couple of months at a time, but Neill never lost a night's sleep over them. Eventually, he found, most of them settled down and got to work, but if they didn't he still didn't worry.

The students at Summerhill range in age from about five or six to sixteen or seventeen. They may enter or leave at any time. Most remain about seven years. The number of students varies, but usually there are between fifty and one-hundred, a fair percentage of them from the United States and countries other than England. There has been no systematic follow-up of the alumni of Summerhill (there are no "graduates") but a series of interviews with men and women who had spent some time there revealed mixed reactions.

As is probably true of any other school, some liked it and some didn't. Some thought their experience at Summerhill was very helpful with their overall developments; others weren't so sure, or thought just the opposite. Some said they would like to send their own children there (but very few did); others said they would not. In general, what they liked best about Summerhill was the atmosphere of warmth, acceptance, and the opportunity they had to develop a healthy attitude toward sex. Their main complaint had to do with what they considered to be an inadequate academic program and incompetent teachers. Most of those interviewed thought that a few years at Summerhill for children under the age of ten would be fine, but much more than that, especially for older children, would probably not be wise. Despite the lack of evidence or even testimony that Summerhill has been any kind of a smashing success, it continues to fascinate the romantics who hold it up as an ideal school, a model of what good education should be.

OPEN CLASSROOMS

More frequently imitated in the United States than Summerhill have been the British primary schools, the prototype of the open classroom. Several versions of open classrooms have been instituted in the United States since the early 1960s, some more open than others, each likely to be somewhat different from any other one. Since the whole point of the open classroom is flexibility, spontaneity, and informality, there can be no formula for its organization or very specific methodology for its operation.

In England, where they've been working since the late 1940s, as in the United States, an open classroom is most immediately and obviously distinguished by its physical appearance. There are no desks bolted to the floor, no chairs arranged in neat rows. A child has no assigned seat and is not expected to be in any particular place at any particular time. He is, rather, free to spend his time at a "station" or work area of his choice. Several such stations are available, some of which may be located in the corridor, another room, or out of doors. Each station has its appropriate furnishings and materials.

In the reading area, for example, there are a number of books at different levels of difficulty, a few comfortable chairs and maybe a rug to lie on. In the math area there is a collection of mathematical puzzles and games, workbooks, measuring instruments, objects to be counted or weighed, Cuisenaire rods, and that sort of thing. At the science station, there are rocks, fish, plants, birds, some small animals, leaves, shells, bulbs, batteries, etc. Other stations are equipped for art and music. Also likely to be found are facilities for water play, a sand box, building materials, and some other things which I've probably overlooked.

Students are free to go from one area to another as they please, to work alone or in small groups. There are no bells or timetables. One of the few requirements in the British schools is that every child spend some time every day reading, but what he reads and when, is up to him. Other requirements are that the child must clean up after himself and return things he has used to their place, and that he must not interfere with another child's work. Otherwise, he's pretty much on his own. The teacher rarely, if ever, talks to the entire group at the same time, nor does she spend much of her time at her desk. Rather, she acts as a kind of roving resource person, offering help when she is asked, but otherwise not intruding.

The British "open" schools were originally intended for children between the ages of five and seven, but some of its features have been extended upward and modified for use with older children, as has been done in this country. On at least one point, observers of open classrooms in the United States as well as England agree: the kids seem to love it.

FREE SCHOOLS

Not to be confused with open classrooms, or with freedom schools, are so-called free schools. Open classrooms are to be found, with varying degrees of openness, as part of the established public or parochial school systems in all parts of the country where they have been operating with varying degrees of success. They can also be found in many nonpublic or nonparochial independent schools which are of neither the "free" nor "freedom" variety. Freedom school was the name given to private institutions created in the late 1960s and early 1970s to avoid racial integration which had been mandated by the courts. Already pretty much historical relics, these tended to be quite conservative in educational as well as political and social philosophy. In no sense were they "open" and they certainly were not intended to promote the kind of pupil freedom in which the romantic reformers were interested. Free schools were also private institutions established and financed for the most part by parents of a much more liberal persuasion who accepted the romantics' criticisms of the existing public school systems and wanted to implement their recommendations for reform.

In addition to their being privately supported and independent of the regular public school systems in their districts, free schools were likely to be even less structured than an open classroom and to allow children even more freedom. While emphasizing freedom and individuality, the open classroom assumes that children are there to learn something rather specific, such as the 3 Rs and certain types of subject matter, which accounts for the presence of reading and mathematics areas, science stations, and the like. Children are free to work at the area of their choice, but they are expected to work.

It is impossible to say exactly what free schools were like because every one was different. But generally speaking, they operated on the lines of Summerhill. They did not intend to teach anyone anything in particular, but tried to provide an atmosphere of freedom and love in which every pupil would experience happiness and achieve a high degree of personal fulfillment. They were typically staffed by idealistic but incompetent young people, with beautiful visions but few skills, who were perhaps as much concerned with trying to find themselves or to register their protests against the established way of doing things as they were with educating children.

Much given to such activities as rapping, guitar playing, and weaving head bands, these "teachers" felt that the development of the child's personal feelings and social relationships took precedence over the development of his intellect. When the child felt ready to learn how to read, they assumed that somehow he would learn—informally, without systematic instruction, but with perhaps a little casual assistance from one of the staff.

The only problem was that a great many free school students did not learn how to read, nor did they learn much else as far as their parents could see. Dissatisfied with their regular public schools, many of these parents were apparently even more dissatisfied with the free schools. At any rate, they withdrew their children as well as their financial and moral support.

I have, incidentally, been using the past tense in writing of free schools, not because the movement is dead, but because literally hundreds of such schools which were founded in the United States since the mid 1960s or so are no longer in existence, most of them having survived for less than two years.

DISCOVERY AND PERSONAL MEANING

The open classroom as well as other forms of student-centered education presuppose that the only worthwhile kind of learning is that which results from the individual's own discovery and which has personal meaning to him. The ideas of "meaning" and "discovery," in fact, are practically inseparable, and in rather sharp contrast to conventional methods of teaching. Traditionally, our schools have operated on the basis of "expository" teaching and "receptive" learning. Teaching is equated with giving, learning with receiving. Having decided what her students should learn, the teacher presents the material to the students in what she regards as a logical well-organized manner, expecting that it will thus eventually come to make as much sense to them as it does to her. The expectation, in other words, is that they will come to perceive it as she does. The teacher might further try to "make" the material meaningful to the students, or "give" the material meaning by explaining how it relates to them now or how they might be able to apply it in the future.

Humanistic educators are much more favorably disposed to the *discovery method* of teaching and learning. Here, insofar as possible, the student learns through his own efforts and arrives at his own meanings with a minimum of teacher explanation or intervention. He relies, to a much greater extent than in a conventional classroom, on his own observations and activities, his own processes of experimentation and inductive reasoning. In this situation, asking the right questions is more highly regarded than giving the right answers. Being able to figure something out for oneself and knowing where to find needed information is more valued than having that information at one's fingertips or stored away in one's memory.

Learning by discovery is supposed to have several advantages over the more passive method of learning. It is, for example, supposed to help the student learn how to learn, and how to acquire information he might need in a given situation. It is supposed to develop his curiosity and sharpen his powers of reasoning. It is supposed to make him more self-reliant, and less dependent upon his teacher or his textbook. It is supposed to lead to better retention and greater possibilities for application. It is supposed to involve the student more actively in his own education and give him a greater responsibility for it. It is supposed to be a lot more fun than sitting and listening, note-taking and reciting. It is also supposed to make one's learning a lot more personally satisfying and meaningful. It has not been conclusively demonstrated that all of these suppositions are valid, but there are some grounds for believing that they are.

The "meaning" of a subject, as that term is used here, refers to an individual's perception of the implications of that subject, its relationship to other subjects, its significance to him here and now or in the future. As we noted earlier in our discussion of perception, the meaning of some particular fact or principle or theory to a person depends on his existing interests, needs, values, and goals; on what he has previously learned and presently remembers or believes about the subject; on his level of maturation, his particular circumstances, and a number of other variables. These ideas, of course, tie in with the notion that learning is necessarily a highly personal matter and that meaning is something that cannot be given, but must be derived by the person himself for himself.

TEACHERS AND THEIR METHODS

Countless methodology textbooks are readily available abounding in specific suggestions for using the discovery, as well as other, methods of teaching, but humanistic educators are likely to take a dim view of them. They just can't get excited about techniques. Their position is that there is no formula for good teaching, no bag of tricks that is guaranteed to work or double your money back; no one best way of managing a classroom or organizing a learning experience. Teaching, they feel, is not a science or a branch of technology; it is, rather, a creative art involving a personal relationship between unique individuals. If a teacher is to help a student develop his individuality, she must express hers. She must draw on her own background since she cannot draw on anyone elses. She must use her abilities and her resources, her perceptions, her imagination, her previous experience, her unique combination of personal characteristics and potentialities. She must discover for herself the methods that are likely to be most effective in helping her particular students in this particular class. Methods that were successful with others might fall flat with this year's students. The teacher in a humanistic school, therefore, must be highly flexible, familiar with a variety of possible procedures, but bound by none of them. Because they regard her as much more than a dispenser of knowledge or a conveyor of the cultural heritage, and because of the common connotations of the word *teacher*, they are likely to eschew that term and refer to her as a "facilitator" and to her job as a "helping relationship." They are also likely to be far more interested in her personal qualities than her skills or competencies. A good teacher, from this standpoint, cannot be so readily identified by what she does as by the kind of person she is. A good teacher is not a cold, efficient robot, but a warm, friendly, sympathetic, understanding human being. She is an authentic person who does not pretend to be what she is not. She accepts herself and is therefore able to accept her students. And, of course, she accepts humanistic psychology.

MOTIVATION

One of the most distinctive characteristics of humanistic education is that it is based on intrinsic as opposed to extrinsic motivation. Extrinsic motivation involves the use of some incentive, some promised reward, or some threat of punishment, that emanates from outside the individual himself. A person who works at his job primarily for the financial remuneration or who pays his taxes to avoid having to go to jail is extrinsically motivated or outer directed. So is a child who studies his mathematics in order to get a good report card mark or a place on the honor roll, or to please his teacher or avoid a scolding from his parents. Such traditional educational incentives, which often involve competition, arbitrary standards, and perhaps an element of fear, have at times proved to be highly effective from the standpoint of scholastic achievement. But they hardly constitute the ideal. Humanists decidedly prefer intrinsic motivation, inner direction, or a system of education based on the student's interests.

Intrinsic motivation occurs when a person recognizes the value inherent in a particular activity and regards the activity as a desirable end in itself. The activity is self-rewarding; it is interesting; the person derives satisfaction from the very process of engaging in it. A good example of intrinsically motivated behavior is play. Ordinarily, parents or teachers do not have to motivate children to play. Children, and for that matter adults, play because they want to, because they like to. It is in this sense and for this reason that humanists would like to model education after play, rather than work, and make of it a pleasant experience in which pupils might freely and happily choose to participate.

This is not to say that humanists want to try to make education all fun and games—although some of them might ask, "Why not?" Nor are humanists opposed to students' setting forth a great deal of effort. Enjoyment does not preclude hard work, nor does interest in an activity rule out effort. On the contrary, the more intrinsically motivated a person is, the greater the effort he is likely to expend.

Humanists, you will recall, believe that children naturally want to learn, and that there is no need to bribe them to do so or to threaten them if they don't. What distresses the humanists is that children are so often forced to learn things that they do not especially need to learn and do not particularly want to learn when there are so many other interesting and exciting things that they could be learning and would like to learn. What are some of these things? According to the humanists, the only way to find out is to ask individual students. That's why they're all for student-centered education.

Even in our most traditional schools, teachers ordinarily try to arouse and maintain students' interest in the subjects they are teaching. But there's the rub. They begin with the subject they are teaching rather than the people they are teaching. They try to "sell" their subject, to create an interest where one does not exist, to convince their students of its value, to persuade them that it's worth studying. If a teacher believes that her job is to transmit the good old cultural heritage, what else can she do? But if she conceives her job to be along the lines I have been sketching, humanists claim the problem practically disappears.

For the humanist, motivation as such is not a special problem that precedes learning. It is, rather, an integral part of the total learning process. Motivation, then, is largely a matter of offering the student a variety of activities in which he already has some interest; activities out of which newer and deeper interests can be expected to grow; activities based on his natural inclinations to explore, experiment, manipulate, and communicate; activities which he will be able to perceive as means of helping him achieve his goals; activities which he will find enjoyable and worthy of his efforts.

SOCIALIZATION

Their emphasis on the individual notwithstanding, humanistic educators recognize that the school is a social institution with a social purpose. They recognize that individuals do not live or learn or fulfill themselves only as individuals; they can do so only in some particular society. They recognize that schools are established and maintained by a particular society to help young people take a place in that society and contribute to its improvement. The social purpose of the school involves a lot more than helping individuals learn to "get along" with one another. It also includes the learning of reading, writing, arithmetic, and other subjects and skills which are considered necessary for the welfare of society as well as the individual. Humanists would like to have individual students learn these subjects and skills while, at the same time, learning how to relate to each other. They would like the school to fulfill its historic mission of transmitting the cultural heritage while, at the same time, helping each student satisfy as many as possible of his personal, emotional, and social needs. They would like, in other words, to have the schools reconcile the individual's striving for self-actualization with the interests, needs, and values of the society to which he belongs.

For reasons such as these, humanistic classrooms are characterized not only by individualized instruction but also by a great deal of group interaction. Discussions, small-group projects, committee work, flexible ad hoc subgroups, team activities, just about anything that involves cooperation is highly recommended. Humanistic teachers are especially fond of learning experiences in which students work together to determine their own goals, decide on the means they will employ to attain them, and periodically evaluate their progress in terms of standards they have set for themselves and have generally agreed upon.

Proponents of this democratic approach claim that such group endeavors are more effective than the alleged authoritarianism of a teacher-centered classroom in arousing and maintaining students' interest in school work, in fostering their mental health, in promoting their social adjustment, in improving their overall classroom behavior, and in developing such traits as reliability and responsibility, consideration and cooperation. They also feel that this kind of social emphasis provides a healthy balance to what might otherwise become narrow individualism or unsocial self-centeredness. They can point to a number of experimental studies which lend support to their position but, as is so often the case, the evidence is not all in their favor. Still, humanistic educators are convinced of the advantages of cooperation over competition, of democratic over authoritarian classroom leadership, and of students' dialogue over teachers' monologues. They are willing to try just about anything that might help their students learn to share, plan together and work together, listen to one another, respect one another, and help one another.

MENTAL HEALTH

One of the major objectives of schools which operate in accordance with principles of humanistic psychology has to do with the promotion and preservation of the student's mental health. For our present purposes, mental health can be considered as having a positive and a negative dimension. Negatively, mental health is a relative degree of freedom from tensions, anxieties, frustrations, conflicts, feelings of guilt, inferiority, hostility, alienation, and other self-destructive feelings. I say "relative" freedom because no one, of course, is ever completely free of these kinds of feelings.

Positively, mental health implies a favorable self-concept, feelings of affiliation and personal worth, a sense of accomplishment and fulfillment, a feeling of being at peace with oneself and with others. No one ever has these positive feelings fully and completely either. This is just another way of saying that mental health is a matter of degree, that no one enjoys perfect mental health, that there's always room for improvement, and that everyone needs help along these lines, some people more than others. Humanists are convinced that the school has a great opportunity and a corresponding responsibility to provide this kind of help, to foster the positive qualities which have just been mentioned and to alleviate, if not eliminate, some of the negative feelings.

A student's self-concept and the other aspects of his mental health depend to a very great extent, of course, on such factors as his home life and peer group relations, as well as socioeconomic conditions and media, over which the school has little or no control. But his mental health also depends to a considerable degree on his experiences in school, on factors which the teacher can control, on what is done to him and for him and with him in the classroom. Humanists maintain that every teacher can, and should at least try to, make her classroom a warm friendly, emotionally comfortable place in which every student is made to feel that he is important, respected, wanted, and maybe even needed. An ideal humanistic classroom, therefore, is one in which every student has an opportunity to experience success and to satisfy his needs for acceptance, approval, and achievement.

There is no ready-made formula for bringing about a classroom atmosphere that will be conducive to students' mental health, nor can there be any guarantee that a teacher's efforts in this respect, no matter what they are, will bring about the desired results. The important consideration here, as in the case of methodology for scholastic achievement, is not so much what the teacher does, but the kind of person she is. Humanistic psychologists feel strongly that if the teacher herself is an emotionally secure person who respects and accepts herself, she will almost automatically manifest her respect for and acceptance of her young friends in the classroom. If she is consciously aware of her friends' needs for love and esteem, recognition and approval, and has the intention of helping them satisfy these needs, and if she is determined that she will do nothing to contribute to her friends' feelings of guilt, frustration, inferiority, and the like, humanists are confident that she will contribute significantly to her students' emotional well-being, regardless of the particular techniques she might employ.

COUNSELING

No responsible, well-informed person expects a teacher to practice psychotherapy or assume the responsibility for helping students who are seriously "disturbed." A teacher is, however, expected to help identify students who are in need of specialized assistance and to make the necessary referrals. In a humanistically-oriented school, the specialist to whom referrals are made is likely to practice a form of what has been called Rogerian (after Carl Rogers) or nondirective or client-centered counseling. One of the basic assumptions of this system of counseling is that the best way, and probably the only way, to change the behavior of a person who is, say, hostile or withdrawn or has intense feelings of inferiority or deep feelings of depression is to change his self-concept. But only the client himself can do this. Only he can change his own feelings about himself. Only he can come to perceive himself in a new and better light. Only he, in the final analysis, can overcome his own difficulty.

The main task of the counselor, therefore, is not to try to solve the individual's problem, or change his behavior, or supply him with answers, or even to give him advice. It is, rather, to help him improve his image of himself and come to accept himself more fully. The counselor does this by giving the client an opportunity to clarify and express his feelings and perceptions in a completely permissive, nonthreatening atmosphere where he can feel assured of the counselor's unconditional acceptance regardless of what he says.

Nondirective counseling can be thought of as a special form of the discovery method of learning. The assumption is that the client himself, and only the client himself, is capable of discovering the solution to his problem because the solution lies within himself. He needs help, of course, and it is the function of the counselor or therapist to provide this help. But the help does not take the form of telling the person what to do. It is more a matter of helping him arrive at a deeper understanding and a fuller acceptance of himself so that he will be in a better position to make his own decisions and map out his own course of action. As is the case with teacher methodology, only more so, what the counselor says or does, the particular techniques he employs, are not as crucial as the kind of person the counselor is. The client's improvement depends on his coming to terms with himself and learning to accept himself. To learn to accept himself he must feel that he is accepted with no strings attached, no ifs, ands, or buts, by another person whom he regards as significant, in this case the counselor. The counselor's acceptance of the client must be genuine. If the counselor pretends to accept the client, whereas, in fact, he rejects him or is annoyed with him or is intent on threatening him, the value of the relationship is destroyed. In order to accept another person honestly and unconditionally, a counselor (or for that matter anyone else) must first arrive at an unconditional acceptance of himself—which means that from the humanistic standpoint the counselor must be, if nothing else, a secure, authentic, well-intentioned person.

MORAL EDUCATION

Along with mental health, another major objective of humanistic education is to develop moral autonomy, which is one of the essential aspects of self-actualization. The morally autonomous person acts in accordance with moral principles which he understands, has thought through and evaluated, and has come to accept as his own. He acts as he does in moral situations not to impress others or to avoid censure or for any other extrinsic reason, but because he believes it is right for him to do so and he freely chooses to do so. His moral principles are relatively stable and his behavior is consistent with those principles, but he is not rigid in the way he applies them to particular situations. His principles, moreover, are subject to modification as new insights, deeper understandings or broader experience might recommend. He deliberates before acting, taking into account the feelings and welfare of others. Perceiving no dichotomy between his own good and that of his fellow man, he is able to act in a socially constructive and acceptable manner while, at the same time, being true to his own inner convictions. This is the type of person humanists would like to see our schools help develop.

Since they believe in man's capacity for and right to self determination or freedom of choice, and man's inherent goodness and tendencies toward moral perfection, and the relativity of moral standards and values, humanistic educators maintain that moral autonomy (or good character, if you prefer) cannot be taught in the sense that mathematics and science can be taught. It can only be learned, as mathematics and science are best learned, through the individual's own private act of discovery. They feel that it is not only ineffective but actually wrong for one person to even try to impose his values on someone else or decide for him what he should or should not do in a given moral situation. They feel that this is too much like trying to play God, and that it constitutes a violation of the other person's freedom and individuality and even his basic humanity.

Far better, humanists believe, to permit and encourage the individual to find his own set of moral values and principles. As is the case with other kinds of teaching, there is no one best way to provide the student with the help he needs in this area. But providing this help is largely a matter of developing his ability to think critically and responsibly about moral problems. It also involves such things as meeting his social and emotional needs and giving him opportunities to learn how to make important decisions.

Dewey

Moral education to a humanist does not imply indoctrinating the student with a predetermined code, and it certainly does not involve bribing or threatening or begging or persuading him to behave in a predetermined manner. It does imply respect for his freedom, dignity, and natural tendencies toward socialization, as well as an honest attempt to help him understand, compare, and evaluate a variety of possible moral positions. Ultimately, only he can decide for himself which he wants to choose as a guide to his own behavior. No self-respecting humanist would deliberately set out to "teach" morality formally and systematically, but then neither would he formally set out to "teach" science or mathematics either. He would, however, try to miss no opportunity to help a student learn moral principles, and if the choice had to be made between helping him learn mathematics or morality, would in all probability opt for the latter.

COMPULSORY SCHOOL ATTENDANCE

Most of the critics and reformers in the romantic-humanistic camp believe that schools are here to stay, that they have a tremendous potential for improving the quality of life in our society, but that they are for the most part greatly in need of renovation. They believe that the kinds of practices and principles we have been considering should be implemented in more of our schools on a much larger scale as a means of bringing about the necessary improvements. But a minority of this group have suggested that the schools as we know them are beyond repair. Such critics as John Holt, Ivan Illich, and Paul Goodman, among others, have suggested that mere patching up jobs through curriculum changes and administrative innovations are insufficient, that the traditional school has outlived its usefulness, and that a major overhauling of the entire educational system is in order. As part of this overhauling, the school might be recognized as one, but only one and not necessarily the most important educational agency, and the whole concept of compulsory school attendance would have to be reexamined.

Apart from any philosophical or psychological considerations, a legal question has been emerging as to whether compulsory school attendance laws might not be in violation of the United States Constitution. At least a few reputable authorities on the Constitution believe that they are, and at least a few recent federal court decisions upholding the rights of children and their parents in school-related cases would seem to support their position. In addition, there is the well-known financial plight of our educational system and the unwillingness of the public to sanction ever-increasing taxes to cover ever-increasing costs of the schools, especially after having been told by the romantic reformers how bad the schools are.

Even if ample money is found to continue our present system of universal compulsory school attendance, and even if compulsory attendance requirements are not found to be unconstitutional, the questions remain: Are schools really so essential that everyone should be forced to attend one? Is it not time we recognized that compulsory education is really impossible, and that compulsory school attendance might not contribute very much to one's education at all? Might there not be better ways to provide for the education of the young than forcing them to spend twelve years or more in one of those allegedly grim, joyless, outmoded, opppressive, irrelevant, de-humanizing, concentration camps known as schools, where dreams are killed and minds are mutilated?

A few of the more romantic romantics, who still haven't given up on the free school idea, have proposed that the entire system of compulsory school attendance be abolished and that no child be required to attend any school ever. More numerous, but still in a minority, are those who would retain compulsory school attendance for those up to about the age of 12, or 14 at the most, with a variety of alternatives for those beyond that age.

ALTERNATIVES

I will not attempt to describe all of the alternatives to the traditional junior-high and high school that have been proposed. I couldn't if I wanted to because I'm sure that some alternatives have been suggested which I have either never heard of or have forgotten. But here are some of the options that would be available to boys and girls in their teens if some of the roman-tics, as well as certain unromantic, hard-headed critics, had their way.

For those who wanted it, particularly for college prepara-tory purposes, there would be the conventional academic high school. Its program could be reduced to two years or less, but those who wanted to attend longer could do so. For others, there would be more and better technical or vocational schools whose programs would be practically oriented toward some particular occupation and where academic subjects would be taught if and when and as they were needed for that purpose. There would also be many more apprenticeships, work-study programs, co-ops, and opportunities for in-service, on-the-job training in offices, stores, factories and elsewhere, with business, industry, and organized labor assuming a large part of the responsibility for such programs.

There would be more continuation schools which young people could attend on a part-time basis, days or nights, to take courses they wanted, when they wanted, for purposes of job upgrading, or toward a diploma, or simply for their own personal satisfaction. Perhaps they would be paid for attending classes or released from their jobs for a few hours a week to do so.

There would also be "free schools," tuition free as well as free in the sense of there being no requirements, tests or grades, where young people (and older people as well) could come anytime to learn just about anything they might be interested in from astrology to Zen. The students would plan and operate these schools, which would not have to be housed in a school building. Not only these free schools but the more structured conventional schools as well would hold some of their classes in a student's or teacher's home, or at a library or museum or YMCA or a tavern or out on the grass in a park or wherever.

In addition to these different kinds of schools, there would be a number of learning centers in various parts of the community where a person would have easy access not only to books and magazines, but to films, slides, tapes, projectors, teaching machines, computers, closed-circuit TV, and whatever other mechanical or electronic equipment might be available. Trained staff members would be on hand to help him learn to use this equipment as a means of his teaching himself whatever he might want to learn at his own convenience.

An attempt would be made to involve as many different kinds of people as possible in the educational process. Not only professionally-certified teachers but housewives, factory workers, retirees, businessmen, and young people themselves would be invited to teach whatever they happened to know that someone else wanted to learn: a foreign language, automobile mechanics, chess, guitar-playing, pie-baking or what have you. This teaching could be done in one of the school buildings, of course, but it might be better if done in someone's home or shop to maintain an atmosphere of informality.

COMMUNITY SERVICE PROJECTS

Another kind of alternative to compulsory high school attendance which an individual could select along with any of the options that were just mentioned would involve him in some sort of community service project. As we noted in the first chapter, young people of today want and need genuine responsibilities and opportunities for productive action but many do not have them in their homes, their schools, or anywhere else. Hence, their feelings of alienation, frustration, aimlessness, uselessness, boredom, and the like.

The suggestion is being made with increasing frequency that, perhaps under the sponsorship of the school, ways be found to permit people in their teens to begin to function as responsible, productive members of their community; that ways be found to involve them in worthwhile activities with adults, to help both learn to understand and work with one another, instead of isolating them from one another, culturally if not physically, as is presently done; that ways be found to give the young person the feeling that he is doing something important to help other people and to make his community a better place in which to live.

It seems paradoxical that there is so much work to be done in our communities that is not being done while, at the same time, teenagers are looking for something important to do but can't seem to find it. There is so much that could be done, for example, to clean up our streets and alleys and parks and streams and keep them clean, or to help patients in hospitals and nursing homes and old people, sick people, handicapped people, retarded people, not to mention the many younger children who need someone to care for them or play with them or maybe tutor them.

Some young people have, of course, been engaged in these kinds of activities on a voluntary basis for years. The suggestion under consideration is that many more young men and women be given much more time and encouragement and opportunity to render these kinds of services, not simply as something they do in their spare time, but as a significant, integral aspect of their overall education. Perhaps they could be paid a reasonable amount of money for their services. Perhaps they could spend twenty hours a week or so on these kinds of projects and still find time to attend some kind of school or other. Perhaps the school could coordinate these activities, but the students themselves would have the major responsibility for planning, organizing, carrying out, and evaluating their projects. They would also have the responsibility for thinking of new and better projects to which they could devote themselves.

The possibilities in this regard are practically without limits, and the benefits to the community, as well as the participating individuals, potentially far greater than our present system of compulsory school attendance. So, at least, the de-schoolers maintain. But community service projects are only one of several alternatives that could be offered as a means of helping to bring about a fully humanistic educational program.

Get kids involved in out of school experiences that enable them to evaluate themselves and at the same time give them the opportunity to learn traditional methods.

HUMANISTIC EDUCATION

All of the proposed alternatives to compulsory school attendance which have just been mentioned are being used, at least on a small scale, in various parts of the country, and the search for other alternatives continues. But neither alternatives as such nor the reduction, much less elimination, of compulsory school attendance is essential to the humanistic position. As a matter of fact, those whom we referred to in the first chapter as conservative critics, as well as a number of behavioristic educators and psychologists, are among those seeking alternatives to the conventional high school.

Far more basic to humanistic education are such concepts as intrinsic motivation, human dignity, individualization and socialization, discovery and personal meaning, human potentialities, man's inherent goodness, responsibility, flexibility, self-concept, feelings and perceptions, and, of course, freedom and self-actualization. Before attempting to evaluate educational programs which are based on these concepts, let's see what the behaviorists have to offer.

4

Behaviorism

*Good People
Don't Just Happen.
They're Produced.*

Behaviorism goes back to the 1920s, and earlier than that if you care to trace remote geneologies. It is so called because of its underlying assumption that the only thing that can be known about a person with any degree of certainty is his overt, observable behavior and that such behavior is the only legitimate subject matter of psychology. Its acknowledged founder, John B. Watson, believed that psychology, the study of human behavior, could be and should be based exclusively on the same rigid scientific principles and methodology that had been used so successfully in such disciplines as physics, chemistry, and biology. Only that which could be examined under laboratory conditions and which lent itself to scientific analysis was valid data for the psychologist. Thus, Watson rejected such concepts as mind, intellect and will, feeling, desire, and consciousness, as well as subjective introspective experiences which cannot be objectively verified or put to any kind of scientific test. Nor was there any room in his system for speculation about human nature or anything else.

Watson and his followers assumed that all human behavior, including the most complex of man's activities, could be explained in terms of conditioning. In this respect, man was held to be essentially no different from lower forms of animal life. A person behaves as he does because he has been conditioned to do so. His so-called purposes or intentions or inclinations are irrelevant. His behavior is not caused by any "motives" arising from within, but is determined by external forces over which he might have little or no control. Even what had been previously thought of as distinctively human acts—thinking, willing, and loving—are really nothing more than the consequences of the individual's prior patterns of conditioning. Behaviorism has undergone some significant revisions since the 1920s, but these assumptions are still generally held by many behaviorists of the 1970s.

Third force psychology, as we have seen, developed largely as a reaction to what were perceived as the materialistic, mechanistic, deterministic, dehumanizing elements of early behaviorism. Those who came to be known as humanists could not accept the behaviorists' assumption that man is no more than a highly developed beast—or a very complex piece of machinery. They could not agree that a human being could be fully understood, much less appreciated, by sole reliance on the methodology of the physical sciences. They could not buy the behavioristic notion that education is essentially no different from animal training, a matter of conditioning children to make predetermined responses to given stimuli. And they certainly were unwilling to go along with the behaviorists' denial of human freedom .

BEHAVIORAL ENGINEERING

At about the same time that third force psychology was gaining prominence, newer systems of behaviorism were developing, partly in reaction to what were perceived as the contributions or shortcomings of humanism, and partly as a means of overcoming what were recognized as deficiencies in the older behavioral systems.

The leading figure in what might be termed the behavioristic revival of the late 1960s and early 1970s has been B. F. Skinner. Among the other prominent contemporary behaviorists are David Premack, Arthur Staats, Ogden Lindsley, Merle Meacham Charles Madsen, Donald Baer, Albert Bandura, Robert Mager, Wesley Becker, and Sidney Bijou. Like those individuals who are classified as humanists, these behaviorists are by no means in complete agreement with one another on all points.

They do, however, have enough in common to warrant being grouped together for purposes of discussion.

Because of their interest in developing what they call a technology of behavior, contemporary behaviorists are commonly referred to as behavior "shapers" or behavioral engineers. They have refined the principles and techniques of early behaviorism much as their counterparts in the automobile industry have developed more sophisticated means of producing cars over the last half century or so. Behavioral engineers maintain that human behavior can be improved, much as cars can be improved, using essentially the same approach: the methods of science and advanced technology. Good cars do not come into existence by chance; they do not just happen "naturally"; they are produced. Similarly, good people, however the term *good* is defined in this context, do not just happen to come into being; they are produced. The job of the behavioral engineer is to produce good people.

REACTIONS TO HUMANISM

Most contemporary behaviorists have assimilated into their own systems what they regard as the worthwhile contributions of humanistic psychology. They have, for example, attempted to explain such things as love, purpose, meaning, the self-concept, self-determination, and self-actualization in behavioristic terms. But for the most part they consider the views of the humanists and their recommendations for educational reform too vague, too fuzzy, too idealistic, too sentimental, too impractical, too romantic, too unscientific to be of any use. Moreover, they charge that some of the humanistic assumptions are likely to do a lot more harm than good to the individual, as well as society, by making promises, as it were, that cannot be kept. They maintain, for example, that you cannot simply turn a child loose and expect him to "discover" the things he needs to know or do. Parents or teachers simply cannot, in the name of freedom abandon control over their children and expect them to naturally develop into good citizens.

The problems in our schools, according to the behaviorists, do not stem from any lack of pupil freedom, but from a faulty notion of what freedom is. Children do not fail to learn because of too much intervention on the part of the teacher, but because of too little or the wrong kind of intervention. They insist that you cannot simply give children the "opportunity" to grow into well-informed, responsible, creative, independent thinking, morally autonomous, self-actualizing individuals and sit back and wait for them to do so. You, or someone, must teach them how. It is not enough for a teacher to be a "warm, friendly person." She must also be a skilled technician, a behavioral engineer.

BEHAVIOR MODIFICATION

It would be very difficult to talk about behaviorism for very long without getting into the subject of education, because education implies learning and learning is what behaviorism is all about. One of the basic assumptions of behaviorism is that, except for a few simple reflex actions and primary drives, all behavior is learned. The term *behavior* as used here refers not only to one's overt activities, but to his internal activities as well; not only to what he does physically, but also to how and what he feels, believes, understands, thinks, values, perceives, etc.

According to our behavioristic friends, a person's habits, attitudes, predispositions, and tastes are not innate nor do they grow out of his "human nature." They are acquired as a consequence of his contact with his environment, particularly his interaction with other people. So are his likes and dislikes, his preferences and prejudices, his fears and anxieties, his interests and inclinations, his goals and most of what he considers to be his needs. So are his self-concepts and his adjustment patterns, his personality traits and his character. Unsocial and antisocial behavior, neurotic and much psychotic behavior, self-diminishing and just plain stupid behavior, as well as more desirable forms of behavior, are all learned responses. All of these kinds of behavior, moreover, are learned in essentially the same way, through some form of conditioning. Thus, education, according to the behaviorists, is a process of conditioning people to make "desired" responses—to modify and hopefully improve their behavior.

Many people have a hard time with this concept of education as behavior modification or human engineering. "What right," they demand, "does any person have to try to change another? Why can't we just let people be themselves instead of programming them to be something else?" A behaviorist might respond somewhat as follows:

> If you are perfectly satisfied with the world as it is and see no room for improvement or no problems in need of solution; if you are completely satisfied with yourself and the behavior of everyone with whom you come in contact; if you cannot conceive of people being happier, better informed, better adjusted, or more honest, coopera-tive, and compassionate than they are; if it doesn't bother you that many people are poor, ignorant, lonely and oppressed or depressed, or greedy or cruel or incompetent, and you really want to leave them as they are; if you wouldn't mind having kids come out of school at age eighteen no different intellectually or socially from what they were when they entered at age six; in short, if you're sure you don't want to change anybody in any way whatsoever, or if you don't care about the direction in which people change, then behav-iorism doesn't have much to offer you. But then neither does any college or university.

But, the behaviorist might continue, if you are interested in growing, developing, maturing, in expanding yourself or in achieving what you might call fulfillment or self-actualization; or if you are interested in helping others do so; or if you are concerned with helping to make your community or your planet a better place in which to live; or if you have ever wanted to learn anything or to teach anyone anything, then rid yourself of the sophomoric notion that there's something abhorrent about trying to change people and recognize that only through behavioral change can any of your goals, or anyone else's, ever be achieved.

THE PURPOSE OF EDUCATION

Strictly speaking, behavioral engineers are not concerned with changing people, but with changing their behavior. Even more strictly speaking, they are not as concerned with changing people's behavior as they are with producing environmental stimuli which will bring about, or at least increase the probability of, improved human behavior. There's really nothing profound or esoteric about all this. The environmental stimuli to which the behaviorists refer turn out to be such commonplace things as schools, books, curriculum guides, audiovisual aids, lesson plans, and other materials or techniques a teacher might employ. The desired modifications in behavior are nothing more than the ability to read, write, spell, operate a typewriter, speak a foreign language, drive a car, throw a basketball through a hoop, or something of the kind that schools have been concerned with for years.

So the purpose of education, from the behavioristic standpoint, is really very simple and quite traditional: to teach students certain specific predetermined concepts or skills or values or attitudes or other "new and better" ways of behaving, internally as well as externally. The assumption is that there are concepts, skills, etc. which are worth learning and which can be taught. There is no necessary implication here that everyone learn the same thing or that all students learn it at the same pace. There is, however, the implication that the teacher, or the adult society which pays her salary, has a rather clear notion of the kinds of educational objectives students should be expected to attain. This whole matter will be dealt with at greater length in the next chapter, particularly in the sections dealing with "objectives."

PRECISION TEACHING

Teaching, to a behaviorist, implies more than "facilitating" the learning process. It implies more than offering help when asked, more than providing an environment in which the student can learn what he wants when he wants, more than simply informing the student that he is responsible for his own education, more than offering psychological support and physical resources in the hope that the student will somehow discover for himself something of importance. From this standpoint, the teacher does not simply teach children, period. She teaches them *something.* Whether this something be subject matter or personal adjustment or discipline or moral autonomy or an appreciation of music or the fine points of blocking and tackling, teaching to a behaviorist implies conditioning.

Critics of behaviorism profess to be repelled by the very idea of conditioning or training or programming people or of even attempting to "produce" a human being who will fit a predetermined set of specifications. They accuse behaviorists of trying to turn out robots or of wanting to brainwash people so that they will think and do what the "mind manipulators" want them to do. Perhaps a big part of the difficulty here is semantical. If the terms educate, instruct, or facilitate learning were used instead of condition, the whole system might be considerably more palatable to some of these critics. Many behaviorists favor the term "precision teaching." But changing the terminology does not change the nature of the process by which behaviorists claim individuals learn or are taught. Nor does it alter the fact that conditioning procedures have been used by tyrants and would-be tyrants for evil purposes of indoctrination. But from this fact it does not follow that a teacher who conditions a student to believe that 5 x 6 = 30 or that all men are brothers or that Lansing is the capital of Michigan or that heroin is harmful is acting as a tyrant or brainwashing her students or making robots out of them

The term *conditioning* is new as far as the history of education goes, and the term operant conditioning is even newer. Discoveries are still being made about how conditioning works and how it can be used more efficiently in the educational process. But, behaviorists maintain, operant conditioning is essentially the procedure that effective teachers have been using for centuries. By their own admission, behaviorists have not invented a new method of teaching any more than they have a new purpose of education. What they have done is described as precisely and scientifically as they could the traditional method of teaching, refined some age old techniques, and offered some suggestions as to how they think the teaching process can be made even more efficient.

CLASSICAL CONDITIONING

Perhaps at this point we should clarify the distinction between two kinds of conditioning: classical and operant. Classical conditioning, which is also called *respondent conditioning,* is most closely associated with Ivan Pavlov and John B. Watson; operant conditioning with Edward L. Thorndike, B. F. Skinner, and most contemporary behavioral engineers.

Pavlov was a Russian physiologist who won the Nobel Prize for medicine in 1904 for his research on the digestive process. He is not as well known for that achievement, however, as he is for the famous experiment in which he "taught" a dog to drool at the sound of a bell. Pavlov had noticed that as he approached a dog with its dinner, saliva began to flow from the dog's mouth. In the terminology of behaviorism, the stimulus, food, elicited the response, salivation. Both stimulus and response were "unconditioned." As part of the experiment, a bell was rung a few seconds before the food was presented to the dog. The dog salivated, not in response to the bell but to the food. After a dozen trials or so, the bell was rung but no food appeared. Behold, the dog nevertheless salivated. The bell, a biologically inadequate stimulus, had produced the same response that the adequate stimulus had brought about. So closely were the two stimuli associated that eventually the dog came to respond to the bell as he originally did to the food. The dog's reaction to the bell, of course, was a conditioned response.

Applying the same procedures to a human being, Watson conducted his famous experiment in which he conditioned a child to fear a rat. When given a rat to play with, the child manifested no signs of fear whatsoever. Watson had noted previously that young children react with behavior indicative of fear to loud, sudden noises. So just as the child—Albert, by name; age, about eleven months—was about to touch the rat, Watson banged a hammer against a piece of steel, frightening the daylights out of the poor little guy. After this was done a number of times, Albert came to respond to the rat as he had previously responded to the noise.

Watson seems to have gotten carried away. He thought that if he could condition a person to fear a rat, he could condition him to fear anything else. If he could condition a person to fear anything, he could condition him to hate anything. Or love anything. Or do anything. This line of reasoning led Watson to make his well-known claim that given a child young enough and a free hand in training him, he could make of that infant whatever he wished. Watson never even tried to make good his claim, but fifty years later behavioral engineers were at least implicitly making the same kind of claim. In the meantime, parents, teachers, politicians, advertisers, and clergymen, among others, who may never have even heard of Watson have been using the technique which he and Pavlov made famous.

Classical conditioning, which involves the substitution of one stimulus for another and the formation of a strong association between them, can, notice that I didn't say "does," help explain many of the things we have learned, particularly those of a simpler variety. As very young children, for example, we may have been conditioned to respond to the word *chair* much as we would by looking at an object called by that name. Later, we may have been conditioned to respond to the printed symbol *chair* much as we had done to the spoken word. Most of us, I suppose, respond to a red traffic light as we would to a spoken command from a police officer, and we do so automatically, without thinking. We respond to a particular melody as some advertiser wants us to respond, by thinking of the product with which it has been so closely and frequently associated.

We may have been conditioned to associate 1492 with Christopher Columbus so thoroughly that we cannot help recalling the name whenever we hear the date, or vice versa. Perhaps we have been conditioned to respond automatically by saying "you're welcome" whenever someone thanks us or "gesundheit" when someone near us sneezes. We might like or dislike a particular aroma because of certain pleasant or unpleasant experiences we have been conditioned to associate it with. What we do or how we feel in response to such words as fire, God, Republican, Negro, hospital, school, behaviorist, humanism, conditioning, etc., might well be the consequence of our previous Pavlovian experiences. And so on, ad infinitum.

OPERANT CONDITIONING

The key principle of contemporary behaviorism is not classical, but operant conditioning. Operant, or as it is often called, *instrumental,* conditioning is based on the Law of Effect, formulated in the early 1900s by Edward L. Thorndike. Thorndike, incidentally, is credited with being the father of educational psychology because he wrote some of the first books on the subject, taught some of the first courses in the area, and did a great deal of pioneer research on learning and related problems in an attempt to apply psychology to the field of education.

His Law of Effect, simply stated, is that acts having pleasant consequences tend to be repeated and thus learned, while acts having unpleasant consequences tend to be avoided and not learned or unlearned. This law, which underlies the use of incentives, feedback, reinforcement, and the entire system of reward and punishment, has proved to be his most significant contribution to the theory of learning. His discovery of this law was based on research with animals, but let's see how it works with humans.

Suppose that a child is asked, "How much is five times six?" Suppose further that he responds by giving the correct answer. It doesn't really matter why he says "thirty." The only thing that matters is that he does. Maybe 5 x 6=30 was written on the blackboard. Maybe his teacher had just finished telling him that 5 x 6=30. Maybe he did some quick mental addition. Maybe he just guessed. Maybe he had spent considerable time the night before memorizing that fact. No matter. According to the Law of Effect, and what has come to be known as the principle of reinforcement, if he is promptly praised or otherwise rewarded for making that response, by simply being told that he's right, for example, there is a high degree of probability that the next time he is asked that question, he will give the same answer. If the process is repeated often enough, he will learn this bit of information so well that he might never forget it.

But what about the other aspect of the Law of Effect, the matter of unpleasant consequences? Well, suppose that our young friend says that 5 x 6=32. Suppose that he is then scolded, or slapped, or told that he is stupid, or simply that he is wrong, or the teacher's facial expressions register disapproval or the other kids laugh at him. There is a high degree of probability that he won't give that particular wrong answer again. He might say that 5 x 6=11 or 24 or 56 or 10,000; there are, of course, an infinite number of incorrect responses he might give. All that punishment does in a case such as this is eliminate one particular incorrect response or decrease the probability of its recurring. But it does not guarantee that the correct response will be given. Similarly, in home or classroom discipline situations, punishing a child for, say, uttering a particular obscene word might keep him from using that word again, but it will not automatically keep him from using other obscene words nor will it assure his being a model of deportment in other respects. It is for this reason that reward or positive reinforcement is considered to be far more effective than punishment or negative reinforcement in bringing about desired changes in behavior.

In classical conditioning, the consequences of an act are immaterial as far as the learning of that act is concerned. Reward, reinforcement, or feedback are unnecessary. Pavlov did not reward his dog for salivating nor did Watson praise little Albert for cowering at the sight of the rat. In classical conditioning, the stimuli which bring about the desired response are all that matter. These are referred to as *discriminative stimuli.*

In operant conditioning, the consequences or reinforcement of the act is critical. The stimulus which follows the response, the so-called *reinforcing stimulus,* is far more important than that which preceded it. In operant conditioning, only two conditions are necessary for learning or behavior modification to occur: that the desired response be made and that it be followed immediately by positive reinforcement. Incidentally, the word *operant* is just a technical term for the desired response or for a person's so-called voluntary behavior as opposed to his simple reflex acts. The operant is said to be reinforced when the pleasant effect is contingent upon the learner's making the desired response.

REINFORCEMENT

According to the principles of operant conditioning, most human behavior can be pretty well explained only in terms of positive or negative reinforcement. One or another or both of these is indispensable not only to an understanding of one's own behavior but also to the modification of another person's behavior. Let's consider positive reinforcement first.

In animal training, the principal reinforcer is likely to be food—the piece of fish thrown to the seal, for example, when it does its trick, or perhaps petting, as in the case of a dog that does what its master wants it to do. With human beings, a far greater variety of reinforcers may be operative. We ordinarily do not give a child a piece of fish in our culture for behaving properly, but we might give him candy or cookies or a pizza or some other kind of food. We usually do not pet our children in quite the same way that we would pet a dog, but we do hug and kiss and caress them. We might pat the child on the head or, if we happen to be athletes, on the rear end. But the principle is the same. Among other commonly used reinforcers are money, a smile or a word of praise, a gesture of approval or encourage-ment from one's parents or teachers or friends or employers, attention or recognition, the reduction of tension or anxiety, a feeling of strength or power or importance, some tangible object of intrinsic or symbolic worth, a good report card mark, a "warm glow" or an inner feeling of satisfaction, etc.

The exact nature of the particular reinforcer in a given situation, such as that involving the behavior of a criminal or a neurotic or a philanthropist or a saint, may be difficult to identify, but according to the behaviorists, if you look long enough and closely enough, you'll probably find it. But even if you don't, it's still there. The sinner and the saint, the neurotic and the psychiatrist, the teacher and the student, the parent and the child—each did something. It doesn't matter what they did or why or when, but somehow the consequences were pleasant so they did it again. Again their behavior was positively rein-foced and so on until eventually that particular way of acting became habitual. In this way, the behaviorists tell us, they came to think and feel and believe and act as they do.

What constitutes positive reinforcement for one person is not, of course, necessarily reinforcing for another. A piece of whale blubber might be quite an effective reinforcer with an

Eskimo child; an American child would probably respond better to a wad of bubble gum. What is or is not reinforcing to an individual depends primarily on his previous conditioning, on what he has learned to like and want, and on the existing circumstances. The main problem in the practical application of the reinforcement principle, therefore, has to do with finding the most effective reinforcers for particular individuals and with devising "schedules" of when and how much reinforcement should be given.

KINDS OF REINFORCERS

Behaviorists make a distinction between primary and secondary reinforcers. Primary or unconditioned reinforcers are such stimuli as food and drink which are essential to the maintenance of life. The reinforcing power of these physiological stimuli is natural rather than learned. Most reinforcers, however, are of the secondary or conditioned variety. These acquire their reinforcing power by having been associated with or substituted for primary reinforcers. Thus, the smile of a mother as she feeds her child, for example, becomes a secondary reinforcer. Through the conditioning process a spoken word can be substituted for the smile, a gesture or an object for the smile, a word for the object, etc., so that just about anything can theoretically be made a secondary reinforcer.

Certain stimuli, which have been paired with a number of primary and different secondary reinforcers, acquire a general reinforcing effect. Money is one example of such a so-called generalized reinforcer. Attention, approval, and affection, usually referred to as social reinforcers, are other examples. Some stimuli, such as trophies, certificates and report card marks, are referred to as symbolic reinforcers. Certain activities, such as playing a favorite game or watching television, are called activity reinforcers. So a broad variety of reinforcers or potential reinforcers are available.

According to the Premack principle (named for David Premack, who formulated it), any activity that is more attractive to an individual than some other activity has reinforcement potential. If, for example, I like watching football on TV more than I do drying dishes and my wife will allow me to turn on the TV only on the condition that I first finish the dishes, watching the big game reinforces, or increases the probability of, my drying the dishes. A much loftier form of reinforcement might be the feeling of pleasure I derive from helping her. The kiss I receive as a reward might also be quite reinforcing. So might be the prospect of some eternal reward in heaven for my goodness or the pleasant experience of feeling sorry for myself.

Reinforcement, then, can be intrinsic as well as extrinsic. Intrinsic reinforcement refers to activities that are automatically or self-reinforcing. This, in a behavioristic sense, explains interest. No one has to "bribe" me to, or reward me for, watching the football game. Watching it is reward enough in and of itself, and the more I watch the more reinforced I am, the more I want to watch—up to a point, when I become tired of it and extinction begins to set in.

My interest in football (or whatever) is, according to the behaviorists, a learned response, and was probably learned through some sort of extrinsic reinforcement from my peer group many years ago. In understanding the present behavior of a person, behaviorists maintain, it is necessary to take into account the kinds and amount of reinforcement he has experienced. In attempting to modify his future behavior, it is necessary not only to identify the particular reinforcers that will work with him but also to ascertain how much and how often he should be reinforced.

SCHEDULES OF REINFORCEMENT

Behavioral engineers usually classify schedules of reinforcement somewhat as follows:

Continuous schedules are operative in situations when the response is reinforced every time it is made. If the child is picked up whenever he cries, if he is praised whenever he eats his vegetables, if he is told that he's right every time he gives a correct answer in class, he is receiving continuous reinforcement. Intermittent schedules are in effect when the response is sometimes reinforced and sometimes not reinforced. With fixed schedules the response is reinforced in accordance with a kind of predetermined plan based on either the number of responses or the time interval between reinforced responses. If the strategy calls for the child to be rewarded only after he has made the desired response a specified number of times, a fixed ratio schedule is being used. Complementing a child not every time he says "Please" but every fifth or tenth or twentieth time he does so would be an example of fixed ratio reinforcement. If the plan calls for the child to be rewarded for desired responses, regardless of the number of times he makes them, only after a certain period of time has elapsed, a fixed interval schedule is in effect. Taking the child to the movies every Saturday (assuming, of course, that he has behaved himself all week long) would be an example of fixed interval scheduling.

Variable schedules of reinforcement are, in the literal sense, really not schedules at all. Reinforcement is given neither continuously nor in accordance with any hard and fast plan. Rather it varies in an irregular, uncertain pattern. With the variable ratio schedule, the child might make the desired response two or three times before he is noticed; then he might have to make it eight more times before he is noticed again. He might be rewarded after the ninth or tenth response, but then maybe not again until the twenty-fifth or thirtieth. With variable interval schedules, there is the same inconsistency, but with respect to the passage of time rather than the number of responses.

Behavioral psychologists, in classrooms as well as laboratories, but especially in laboratories, have expended a great deal of time and effort attempting to discover which of these schedules is likely to be most effective with which type of learner for which type of learning. They have come up with a number of findings that they regard as interesting, if not important, but humanists by and large are singularly unimpressed. The behaviorists insist, however, that continued research in this area is vital for efficient behavior modification.

AVERSIVE CONTROL

If it isn't positive reinforcement, according to the behaviorists, it's negative reinforcement that explains human behavior. A negative reinforcer is anything that a person finds dissatisfying or annoying, anything that he tries to avoid or escape or terminate or "turn away" from. For this reason, negative reinforcement is commonly referred to as aversive control. It is not quite the same thing as punishment; it is, rather, the avoidance of punishment. It carries with it the implication of "do it or else. . . ."

Behaviorists maintain that historically negative reinforcement has been, and still is, the principal means of social control used by governments, schools, parents, organized religions, and other agencies that want to regulate people's behavior. A person may pay his taxes, for example, not because he gets a rosy glow of satisfaction from doing so or because of a nice thank you note he gets from the Director of Internal Revenue (which would be forms of positive reinforcement), but to avoid having to pay a fine or going to jail. He might work at a dull and distasteful job for eight hours a day to avoid the consequences of not working. A child might clean up his room, to terminate the annoying situation of his mother nagging him. He might study his history to avoid the unpleasantness of failing a history test. He might attend church services regularly to escape the eternal flames of hell. You could, I'm sure, come up with several other examples of negative reinforcement drawn from your own life and the lives of those around you.

One of the major tenets of behavior engineers is that positive reinforcement is potentially a far more effective means of social control than negative reinforcement. They recommend, therefore, that governments, families, schools, and other institutions should concentrate more on rewarding desired behavior and less on threatening punishment for undesired behavior. The concepts of positive and negative reinforcement and punishment as applied to the classroom are discussed at greater length in the next chapter.

BEHAVIORAL THERAPY

One of the first areas in which behavior modification made a great impact is psychotherapy. Some of the most significant work in the behavioristic revival was done in mental institutions and clinics for the treatment of the emotionally disturbed. In fact, behavior modification is still sometimes thought of as a process of using conditioning techniques to overcome "mental illness" or to alter someone's "personality." We have been using the term behavior modification in a broader sense, to include cognitive as well as emotional changes in an individual's behavior. The terms behavior therapy and behavior analysis are used in a more restricted sense to designate attempts at modifying one's emotional or affective behavior.

Behaviorists, of course, assume that a person's fears, worries and anxieties, his feelings of guilt, inferiority, depression, alienation or hostility, his phobias, obsessions, and compulsions are all acquired responses. So, they believe, are drug addiction, dependency on alcohol, one's use of rationalization, compensation, projection or some other defense mechanism, faulty ideas of masculinity and femininity, unfavorable self-concepts and just about everything else that interferes with one's personality adjustment.

Since "maladaptive" or "self-defeating" responses have been learned, behaviorists maintain they can be unlearned or extinguished, and better or more adaptive responses can be learned in their place. The purpose of behavior therapy is to teach clients to make better emotional reponses.

Behavior therapists are not so much concerned with trying to discover the hidden causes of deviant behavior as they are with changing it into more desirable forms of behavior. Thus, they are not greatly concerned with elaborate case histories. They are usually not all interested in trying to probe the client's "unconscious," the very existence of which they are likely to deny. They are inclined to doubt that the underlying causes of, say, hostile or withdrawn or neurotic behavior can ever really be known with any degree of certainty. They doubt, moreover, that an understanding of these causes is even necessary in order to help the client. They have no use for such Freudian concepts as id, ego, and superego, which they regard as mere hypothetical constructs that serve no useful purpose. They feel no particular need for the humanistic idea of the self, which they seem to think only serves to confuse matters. The only thing they care about, and what they prefer to deal with directly, is the maladaptive or deviant behavior itself.

Humanistic psychologists and Freudian psychoanalysts maintain that unless the sources of the deviant behavior are eliminated, the individual's problem is really not solved. Other symptoms, they predict, will eventually emerge or the very same symptoms will crop up again. They insist that it is not enough for a person to merely change, for example, from a withdrawn to an outgoing way of acting. The therapist and the client himself must recognize and come to grips with the underlying causes of the original shyness.

98

Thus, the critics of behavior therapy claim that it deals only with surface behavior, that it treats only the external symptoms of the client's problem, and does not even attempt to get at its roots. Moreover, they claim that behaviorists, in their preoccupation with this surface behavior, overlook the more important matter of the individual's "inner self" and how he perceives himself.

Behavior therapists maintain that the symptoms *are* the problem, and that once the undesired behaviors are extinguished and more desirable forms of behavior are produced, the problem is solved. Their basic procedure, therefore, is to identify the specific undesired behaviors to be eliminated and the desired behaviors to be elicited, and then to use whatever means may be necessary or useful to bring about the intended changes. Behavioral therapy, therefore, is essentially a matter of teaching.

Even more so than is the case with the classroom teacher, the effective therapist must be something more than an understanding, acceptant, well-intentioned "helper." He must be a skilled behavioral engineer with a specialty, as it were, in dealing with emotional disorders. There is no one set method of behavioral therapy; rather, the behaviorist is likely to use any means at his disposal in order to bring about the desired changes. He might lecture, explain, advise, recommend, maybe even insist; he might use individual or group discussions; if he thinks the situation calls for them, he might prescribe drugs or use hypnosis. Most likely, though, he will use some special form of conditioning.

TECHNIQUES

In addition to positive reinforcement, negative reinforcement, and punishment, the following are some of the other techniques and procedures employed by behavioral engineers to elicit desired behaviors or to extinguish those which are undesired:

MODELING: *the process of demonstrating or providing examples of the desired behavior for the learner or client to imitate. Much of a person's behavior is, of course, the result of casual, informal imitation. The teacher might wish to model or present models somewhat more formally and systematically.*

SHAPING: *the process of developing complex behavior by successively reinforcing the parts of, steps toward, or approximations of that behavior. Shaping is essentially a matter of programming and is sometimes referred to as the successive approximation principle.*

SATURATION: *the process of weakening undesired behavior by providing more reinforcement than the individual wants or can stand so that he eventually tires or "gets sick of" the behavior. This process is also referred to as internal inhibition or satiation.*

STIMULUS CONTROL: *the process of regulating or changing the discriminative stimuli to which an individual is exposed, or of controlling the frequency, duration, or intensity of those stimuli. This procedure is most closely associated with classical conditioning.*

CHAINING: *the process of associating a number of simple responses so as to produce more complex behavior. The reinforcing stimulus of one link in the chain serves as the discriminative stimulus of the next. Chaining is used in conjunction with other techniques and is also an element in programming.*

COUNTER CONDITIONING: *the process of reinforcing or developing, through classical conditioning, behavior that is incompatible with the behavior one is attempting to extinguish.*

DESENSITIZATION: *the process of weakening a person's fear of or anxiety about some situation by gradually increasing his exposure to that situation. A feared object, for example, can be presented from a distance and then gradually brought closer, while the client is otherwise comfortable and relaxed. His toleration of the anxiety-producing object is continuously or intermittently reinforced.*

AVERSIVE CONDITIONING: the process of conditioning a person to avoid undesired behavior by presenting or portraying that behavior along with some stimulus that he already finds repellent. Thus he is practically forced to associate cigarette smoking, for example, with vomiting or the agonies of lung cancer.

ETHICAL CONSIDERATIONS

Even the most outspoken critics of behavioral engineering concede that conditioning techniques do indeed work. In fact, they work too well, which is why so many anti-behaviorists are anti-behaviorists. There is not much doubt that through systematic manipulation of the environment, human behavior cannot only be modified but controlled. The problem is: who will do the controlling and who will control the controllers? Thus, the controversy about behavior modification centers, to a great extent, on ethical rather than psychological issues. Great concern has been expressed about the possibility of conditioning techniques being used by unscrupulous individuals for their own selfish ends. Many people are genuinely alarmed about the prospects of "mind control." They are wondering aloud what all of this behavioral engineering is leading to and where it will all end. They keep reminding us that 1984 is really not that far away.

As we have seen, behaviorists do maintain that behavior is shaped, if not determined, by its consequences. This implies that anyone who is in a position to manage or manipulate consequences, that is, to give or withhold rewards and administer punishment, is in a position to regulate and possibly control human behavior. If some small group of individuals were able to gain anything approaching complete control over these consequences and over the stimuli to which people are exposed, they could have something approaching complete control over individual behavior.

Even more alarming than the psychological techniques which behavioral engineers have at their disposal and are constantly supplementing and perfecting is the potential use of biochemistry, psycho-pharmaceuticals, and psychosurgery as instruments of behavior modification or, as some prefer to call it, "mind control." There is no doubt about the possibility of modifying behavior by means of drugs, electrical stimulation of certain parts of the brain, and the destruction or removal of certain neural tissues. The problem is not whether these procedures work. They do. The problem, rather, is whether they should be allowed to work, whether they should even be permitted much less encouraged, whether they can somehow be regulated, and if so, by whom.

The techniques of behavior modification are without question potentially dangerous. Behaviorists hasten to point out, however, that they are also potentially very beneficial . . . if they are used in the "right" way by the "right" people for the "right" purposes. The question remains, what is "right" in this context and who decides? Despite the behaviorists' attempts to allay fears and apprehensions in this respect, anti-behaviorists are still troubled by visions of mad scientists or power hungry politicians out to control the world for their own diabolical purposes.

But surely kind, loving parents and teachers, who want no part of psychosurgery and mind-controlling drugs, are not being diabolical when they use some of the psychological techniques of programming their children at home or in the school. The critics of behavior modification do not question the motives of these parents and teachers. But they are concerned about the future development of the children who are brought up in accordance with the behavioral approach. They fear that these well-intentioned parents and teachers just might be, inadvertent-

I guess I would be an anti-behavioralist for the most part.

ly, of course, inducing a blind kind of conformity and obedience in their children; that they might be inadvertently wiping out their individuality, subtly destroying their concepts of human freedom and dignity, and still inadvertently be preparing them for subsequent mind-controllers whose intentions might be something less than altruistic.

The individual most closely associated with behavioral engineering and the principal target of the anti-behaviorists is, of course, B. F. Skinner. Let's see what he has to say about some of these things.

B. F. SKINNER

Skinner is not only the best known of the contemporary behaviorists but is, according to surveys, one of the most influential psychologists of all time.

Skinner has been fairly well known in psychological circles since the late 1930s when he published his *Behavior of Organisms*. He came to the attention of professional educators in the 1950s largely because of his work with programmed learning and teaching machines. But it was not until 1971, when his controversial book *Beyond Freedom and Dignity* was published, that he became an international celebrity and his name a household term. *Time* magazine did a cover story about him; he appeared on a number of television talk shows; newspapers and popular magazines devoted a large amount of space to his ideas, sometimes in a rather sensationalized manner.

Some of Skinner's readers and listeners have hailed him as a genius who seemed to be offering a blueprint for the alleviation of all human misery and the solution of the world's major problems. Others have perceived him more as a Bela Lugosi-type mad scientist, a refugee from some old old late late movie, out to control the world and transform us all into robots. By his own admission he has infuriated and frightened more people than he has won over. Among those whom he frightened and infuriated was former Vice President Agnew, who labeled him a threat to the concepts of freedom, democracy, individuality, human dignity, and to the whole American way of life.

Skinner visualizes a world in which people can live together in peace and harmony, unhampered by envy, competition, or injustice. He believes that through an appropriate form of education it is possible to bring about societies in which there would be no greed, no crime, no jealousy, no dissatisfaction, no striving for superiority or self-glorification. He describes such a society in his novel, *Walden Two,* a utopian community in which there are practically no social or economic or political problems, where everyone works but no one works very hard or very long, where no one has any fears or anxieties worth mentioning, where everybody is happy and loves everybody else.

This utopia is achieved primarily through a system of education in which everyone is programmed to act as the managers of the community want them to act. Nothing is left to chance. The managers, who are expertly trained as behavioral engineers, carefully control every detail of the total environment. By applying the methods of science and technology to human behavior, they systematically produce the kinds of people needed in order to maintain their society. Far from being robots, as one might imagine, every member of *Walden Two* develops his uniqueness, is inclined toward creativity, expresses his individuality, and to all outward appearances is about as self-actualizing as anyone could possibly be.

Using their ideas, based on extensive research and continuous experimentation, of what is best for the community as a whole, the managers of *Walden Two* decide what people should know and think and value and believe and be able to do. Beginning in early infancy, children are indoctrinated in public communal nurseries where they are reared. The child is never forced to do anything nor is he ever punished. The principal means of control is positive reinforcement. As the child matures, control over his behavior and education are gradually decreased. By the age of thirteen, external controls are eliminated entirely for by that time he has developed "self-control." He has, in other words, been conditioned to want what the managers and adult members of the community want. There is no conflict between his needs or desires and the welfare of his society.

The individual is, in a very real sense, subordinated to society. But Skinner believes that only in a good, well-run society can individuals find happiness and fulfillment and live the good life. The members of *Walden Two* are not, in a sense, free—but then, according to Skinner, neither is anyone else. They at least feel free and are free of aversive controls, which is more than can be said about most of the people in the "outside world." *Walden Two* is, of course, a work of fiction. *Beyond Freedom and Dignity* is a scholarly presentation of the principles that underlie that utopia, and a defense of the basic behavioristic thesis that good men, or good societies, do not just happen, but must be produced.

EDUCATION AND FREEDOM

The purpose of psychology, according to Skinner, is to study man scientifically in order to understand, predict, and control his behavior. In this respect psychology is similar to the physical sciences, the purpose of which is to arrive at a better understanding of the universe in order to predict what will happen under certain circumstances. This knowledge is then used as a means of, if not exactly controlling the universe, harnessing its energies and principles so as to serve man. Those who maintain that if we are able to send men to the moon, we ought to be able to solve the problems of war, poverty, delinquency, etc., have a staunch ally in B. F. Skinner, whether they know it or not, whether they want him as an ally or not.

It's the idea of controlling human behavior that Skinner's critics find most upsetting. They like to think of themselves as free agents, not only capable of regulating their own behavior, but having an inalienable right to do so. But Skinner tells them that their freedom is only an illusion. Their behavior, he insists, is not only influenced but determined by their heredity or their environment or the interaction of the two. He maintains that such words as *will, intention, purpose, goals,* and *desire* do not correspond to anything in reality and are used lamely to "explain" behavior that they cannot explain scientifically.

When asked why you did so and so (anything—use your own example), if your response is something to the effect that you wanted to or chose to, you have explained nothing to Skinner's satisfaction. The question remains, Why did you want to? Why did you choose to do this rather than that? The only reasonable answer in his view, would have to be in terms of your genetic endowment or your environment, including not only present circumstances but also your previous experience and conditioning. Skinner maintains that reliance on the concept of personal autonomy is not only erroneous but actually harmful in that it conceals the real cause of your behavior. We attribute it to something within ourselves and this causes us to ignore the "fact" that actually it is due to something external.

While one's heredity cannot, of course, be changed, one's environment, including the kind of education he receives, can. Thus, if we want to improve ourselves or the behavior of our fellow man or the world around us, Skinner says we must begin by giving up the fetish of freedom. This might at first be a blow to our pride or sense of dignity and personal worth, but only by doing so can we effectively begin the task of producing the kinds of people we want and need. In short, we do not have good people and bad people because some freely choose to be the former and some the latter. We have them because our environment conditions some to act in one way and others in another. So, at least, the behavioral engineers claim.

The task of parents and professional educators and society at large, according to Skinner, is to define the kinds of behavior wanted in their societies and then to produce people who will behave in those ways. Permissive parents and teachers who, in the name of freedom, do not control their children leave them at the mercy of other people or institutions that do control, or at least make a strong deliberate attempt to control, their behavior. For example, authors, film producers, advertisers, disc jockeys, lyricists, politicians, news commentators and editorialists, salesmen, clergymen, peer groups, various special interest groups, dope pushers, and prostitutes, among others, are all trying to exert control over, or shape, people's behavior. All are trying to get people to do something or refrain from doing something.

That which the proponents of personal autonomy might regard as an individual's free choice as to which, if any, of these behavior shapers he will follow is actually the cumulative effect of that individual's previous conditioning plus the relative strength of the reinforcement provided by the particular behavior shapers here and now. Skinner's recommendation is that parents and teachers actively and consciously accept and fulfill their opportunities and responsibilities to shape the behavior of their children and youth in accordance with a carefully thought out, scientifically tested, socially beneficial design. There is, incidentally, no good reason why children and young people should not participate in drawing up this master plan.

THE ESSENCE OF BEHAVIORISM

Not all educators or psychologists or students of psychology who regard themselves as behaviorists accept B. F. Skinner's philosophical assumptions about the nature of man, his lack of freedom and his corresponding lack of any special personal dignity. Nor do they all by any means share his utopian dream. Many card carrying behaviorists see practically insurmountable political and technical and psychological problems in implementing, even on a small scale, the kind of controlled environment or planned society he has depicted. Some see serious ethical problems in even trying to do so. But one need not, of course, accept his political or social views or his philosophical assumptions in order to use the principles and techniques he recommends.

The essence of contemporary systems of behaviorism, as I see it, lies not in rigid adherence to all the views of Skinner any more than it does to those of John B. Watson. Systems of behaviorism have been evolving over the years and, if Skinner will pardon the expression, God willing, they will continue to evolve. In the next chapter, where behavioristic principles are applied to education more directly, behaviorism will be considered in a rather broad sense as embracing the following assumptions: First, whatever the case may be with respect to human nature, human behavior can be improved; second, the purpose of education, be it formal or informal, is to improve human behavior; and third, programming is, if not the only, the most effective way of doing so.

5

Behaviorism
and Education

*How Efficiently Was
Your Behavior Modified
in School Today?*

In contrast to the flexible, spontaneous, permissive, student-centered type of classroom favored by the humanists, behaviorism supports a much more closely structured, carefully controlled, teacher-centered kind of learning environment. As we noted in the preceding chapter, the function of a teacher, according to the behaviorists, is not simply to facilitate the student's learning of what he might at the moment happen to feel like learning. It is, rather, to systematically teach him the subject matter and skills that society expects him to learn.

Behavioristic education is not necessarily committed to the notion of transmitting the cultural heritage in the traditional sense, but it is based on the assumption that teachers and school administrators are able to identify "minimum essentials" of knowledge and intellectual skills which all students should acquire, for their own individual welfare as well as the good of society. The ability to read, write, and compute arithmetically are obvious examples. While a few especially gifted, highly motivated students might be able to acquire these skills on their own, through their personal discoveries or intuition, the vast majority of children will learn them much more efficiently if they are formally taught. Indeed, they might never learn them in any other way. The function of the school, therefore, is to formally, systematically, deliberately teach these skills and whatever else might be considered necessary or important for particular students to learn.

THE TEACHER'S ROLE

The key assumption of behavioristic psychology as applied to education is that the behavior of a learner is determined, not entirely, but to a very great extent, by the behavior of his teacher. What he, the student, learns or does or fails to do depends on what she, the teacher, does and how she does it. The teacher's responsibilities, therefore, are considerably more definite in a behavioristic school than they would be in one conducted along humanistic lines.

To carry out her responsibilities—the word warrants emphasis; that's what they are: responsibilities, and not just "opportunities"—the behavior modifier does not count on the child's "natural tendencies" toward goodness and wisdom because she does not believe he has any such tendencies. She does not excuse her own shortcomings as a teacher on the grounds that the child is, after all, really responsible for his own education because she does not believe that he is. She does not sit back and wait for her pupils to "discover" how to read or spell or add fractions because she thinks hell will freeze over before many of them do so. She does not base her methodology on some romantic notion of the student's freedom because she believes that classroom practices based on that concept are unlikely to contribute to the achievement of her assigned task. She might like fun and games as much as her humanistic cousin does, and she might try to make her classroom as pleasant a place as possible, but she believes that learning involves a certain amount of hard work and discipline. She expects her students to work hard and she works hard herself.

To carry out her responsibilities, the behavioristic teacher believes that she must have a mastery of certain technical skills and professional competencies necessary to bring about the desired modifications in her students' behavior. She believes that she has the authority, and is ready to use that authority, to manage the classroom and control the activities of individual students so that they *will* learn whatever it is that she has been charged with teaching them. She does not fancy herself any kind of autocrat but believes that, if she is to carry out her responsibilities efficiently, she must be pretty well in charge of the whole learning situation. She does not consider herself omniscient, but believes that she knows more about education and her subject matter than her students do.

TEACHER EVALUATION

The main consideration in evaluating teachers, from the behavioristic standpoint, is not whether their pupils like them, or whether they are warm, friendly, sympathetic persons, or whether they are "dedicated," or whether or not they like students or understand them or accept them. Far more important is whether and to what extent their pupils learn what they are expected to learn. Thus, according to the behaviorists, the only really sensible way of evaluating teachers is on the basis of the products they turn out, that is, on the basis of their students' achievement.

The test of a good teacher, like that of a good plumber or physician or baseball pitcher, is purely the pragmatic one of the efficiency with which she gets the intended results. A good teacher is one who turns out good students. A teacher whose students turn out not so good or pretty bad is likely to be judged not so good or pretty bad herself. Failure to learn, behaviorists maintain, is not due to any defect in the student so much as it is to defects in the environment provided by teachers and school administrators. More specifically, faulty learning is a consequence of faulty methods and materials of teaching.

Behavioristic educators are unwilling to attribute a student's poor scholastic achievement to such factors as a lack of motivation or low IQ. They recognize, of course, differences among students in intellectual ability, family background, personal characteristics, etc., and insist that such differences must be taken into account in formulating objectives and in planning the instructional program. They also recognize that variables other than those provided in the school are operative and that teachers are not entirely responsible for what their students do or fail to do.

With proper planning and procedures, behaviorists believe that even so-called slow learners, maladjusted students, disorderly pupils, culturally or economically disadvantaged children and youth, and students with other problems or learning disabilities can be made to learn. Certainly they believe that these as well as normal students can be taught a great deal more than they could possibly learn through some romantic "turn them loose and let them discover for themselves" approach. If they don't, the teacher perhaps should be held accountable.

ACCOUNTABILITY

The concept of accountability in education has been widely discussed since the late 1960s, not so much from the psychological as the economic point of view. It is, however, very much in line with behavioristic thinking. The concept has had a strong appeal to many parents and taxpayers as well as legislators and school board members who are concerned with so-called quality education on the one hand and a shortage of money with which to finance schools on the other. It's generally agreed, or at least assumed, that the quality of a child's education depends on the quality of his teachers. It's also generally known that the biggest single expense of formal education is teachers' salaries.

In recent years, parents and taxpayers, legislators and school board members, have been wondering aloud whether teachers have really been earning their salaries. A teacher's job presumably is to get students to learn. But how much and how well are students learning? Have the billions of dollars spent on education in the United States been spent well? Is society getting its money's worth? Are students getting a quality education? If not, why not? Who's responsible?

Teachers by and large claim that they have been doing a

reasonably good job. But standardized test scores, informal evaluations of students, casual observations, and reports by parents, employers, and students themselves have not always borne them out. When student performance has been found to be less than anticipated, teachers' organizations have tended to blame, if not the child himself or his parents, stingy legislators, unsympathetic administrators and board members, or society at large for its failure to provide the needed financial, as well as moral, support. In return, the argument has been advanced that teachers cannot shift the blame for their own failures on to others, but must themselves be made to account for the quality of their products.

Teachers, it has been charged, are among the few people in our society who are really not accountable to anyone. Factory workers, salesmen, waitresses, business executives, garbage collectors, clergymen, department store clerks, professional athletes, all of these have very specific assigned duties to perform and there is someone in a position of authority to see that they do so. If they don't do their jobs satisfactorily, they may be dismissed and replaced by others who will. Teachers, however, allegedly enjoy tenure and receive their salaries, often with guaranteed annual increments, whether they teach anyone anything or not. All they really have to do is put in their time.

The various systems of teacher accountability which have thus far been developed have not followed any one set pattern. Generally, a committee composed of teachers and administrators, and sometimes parents and board members, draw up a set of objectives specifying what and how much students are expected to achieve in a particular class or at a particular grade level. Standardized tests are used to determine the extent to which those objectives have been attained. If the performance of students is unsatisfactory, in terms of predetermined criteria, an attempt is made to determine why. If the teacher is found to be at fault, some sort of penalty might be in order, but the nature of that penalty, denial of tenure, dismissal, no salary increase, or whatever, usually must be negotiated with the teachers' association.

The whole concept of accountability is based on the assumption that the teacher is responsible, at least in part, for pupil achievement or the lack thereof; that pupil achievement can be accurately, or to use the more technical psychometric terms, validly and reliably, measured; and that the influence of the teacher on pupil performance can somehow be objectively disentangled from other influences on the child, such as his home, peer group, intellectual ability, and socioeconomic background. Not everyone is ready to accept these assumptions. They have been questioned, if not rejected, by the leadership of teacher organizations and humanistic psychologists, among others, but they have received rather strong support from behavioral psychology.

PERFORMANCE CONTRACTS

Closely related to the concept of accountability are the various forms of performance contracts that began to emerge in the late 1960s. At that time, a number of private companies, noting the widespread criticisms of the public schools and the dissatisfaction with the products of those schools, went into the education business. They claimed that, given the amount of money currently being spent on education in a particular school district, they could turn out better products. To back up their claims, they offered contracts to public school systems in which they guaranteed to raise scholastic achievement as measured on standardized tests by a specified amount. If they succeeded, they would be paid an agreed upon fee. If they failed, they would be paid nothing. The contract also provided that the contracting company would select and train its own teachers, provide its own instructional materials, and use its own methods. Typically, they made great use of individualized instruction, teacher aids, incentives, teaching machines, and in general a programming-reinforcing type of methodology.

By the early 1970s well over fifty school districts in

various parts of the country entered into contracts with at least fifty different companies. The results have been generally disappointing and some of the contractors have gone out of business. But some of the more avid proponents of performance contracting are not ready to give up by any means. They maintain that the general idea is sound, but that where they went wrong was in the area of technical details which can and will be corrected. They are convinced that by applying efficiency techniques of business and industry, and by using the best available technology and principles of behavioral engineering, they can bring about better quality education at lower per capita cost than our existing public schools can do.

Whether or not performance contracting will ever catch on and become an important part of the educational system of the future, I certainly don't know. There's a great deal more that could be said for, against, and about the idea. For our present purposes, let us simply note that performance contracting, like accountability, is quite compatible with behavioristic principles of education and human engineering. It is also in accord with the behaviorists' concern, as well as the demands of the public, for greater efficiency and effectiveness in teaching.

BEHAVIORAL OBJECTIVES

One of the main criticisms of education from the behavioristic standpoint is that teachers often are not clear as to what their objectives are. They literally do not know what they are trying to accomplish or what they expect their students to learn. Consider the way educational objectives are commonly stated, in terms of such intended outcomes as, for example, knowledge of history, or understanding of biology, or appreciation of literature, or good citizenship, or critical thinking, or creativity, or personal adjustment, or self-actualization.

Objectives so stated sound nice. They represent lofty ideals and to uninitiated parents or school board members might be quite impressive. But to a behaviorist these objectives are meaningless and potentially harmful. Our behavioristic friends have no quarrel with the intention of these objectives or with the content or skills they are supposed to signify. But they do find fault with the manner in which they are stated. The behaviorist finds that such statements are too broad, too vague, too abstract to be of any help to the teacher or the learner or anyone else. They give the teacher no sense of direction, no idea of where to begin or how to proceed. They give the student no clear idea of what he is expected to do or how he is supposed to do it. There is no way of knowing when or to what extent objectives such as these have been achieved or whether the student is even getting close to achieving them. Such loosely stated objectives, behaviorists claim, reflect fuzzy thinking and inadequate planning. They may be worse than useless in that they cause teachers (and students) to feel that they know where they are heading, whereas actually they do not.

Far more useful, according to the behaviorists, are so-called behavioral objectives. A behavioral objective is a clear, specific description of the desired behavior. It is a precise statement of what the student will do or be able to do as a consequence of the instruction he receives. It is stated in terms of behavior that can be observed and measured so that there is some objective way of determining whether and to what extent it has been achieved.

Some behaviorists are convinced that such outcomes as appreciation of literature, good citizenship, social responsibility, independent thinking and even self-actualization can be taught, just as knowledge of history or understanding of biology can be taught. But first, they believe, the teacher must define these terms much more clearly, not with abstract words or dictionary definitions but with active verbs which denote concrete behavior. She has to identify as specifically as possible, for example, what it is that good citizens do, or what people who appreciate literature do, or what independent thinkers do, or what people who understand biology do.

Then and only then, according to the behaviorists, can she begin to teach her students how to do these things. If she doesn't know or cannot describe what it is that good citizens or independent thinkers do, they maintain, then she cannot teach them to behave as good citizens or independent thinkers. If they do not behave as good citizens or independent thinkers, in no meaningful way can it be claimed that they *are* good citizens or independent thinkers.

KNOWING AS DOING

For centuries it has been assumed that certain bodies of knowledge are indispensable conditions of independent thinking as well as good citizenship. Along with the development of the basic skills referred to as the 3 R's, the most generally accepted objectives of formal education have, therefore, had to do with the transmission and acquisition of knowledge. Let's take history as an example. Somewhere along the line our legislators and educators decided that just about every American student should "know something" about American history. But what, specifically, should he know about it? And what do we mean by *know* in this context?

According to the behaviorists, a teacher cannot simply walk into a classroom and begin to "teach history" all at once. On a given day and at a given moment, she can only teach, and students can only learn, particular facts, concepts, principles, generalizations, theories, interpretations, or particular attitudes, values, impressions or something of that sort. But whatever it is, it must be something in particular. So the problem for the history teacher (or the author of the textbook or the syllabus) is to identify those particulars. Moreover, the behavioristic teacher must describe, in advance, what the student will do as an indication of his knowing or having learned those particular elements. She might, for example, decide that at the end of the term or upon the completion of a unit the student should be able to do the following:

Summarize the provisions of the Missouri Compromise.

Compare the views of Jefferson and Hamilton with respect to a strong federal government.

Define Manifest Destiny.

Name the first five presidents of the United States in the order in which they served.

Identify Samuel Gompers.

Give two arguments for and two against a strong protective tarrif.

Relate three events that led to the Boston Massacre.

Draw a map of the United States showing the land acquired through the Louisiana Purchase.

Explain the Dred Scott Decision.

The possible specific objectives of an American history class are, of course, innumerable and the few examples just given are not necessarily among the best. They do, however, illustrate the kinds of behavioral objectives a teacher might include in her lesson plans. Thus, on a given day she conceives of her responsibility, not in terms of teaching "history," but in terms of teaching, say, the Dred Scott Decision. Her expectation is that at the end of the lesson, her students will "know" that decision well enough to be able to "explain" it.

Behavioristic educators are likely to avoid the use of the words *know* or *understand* in stating their objectives because of the lack of precision in those terms. Instead of trying to define them in the abstract, they attempt to use other, more concrete, verbs such as the following to specify the kinds of desired responses they want their students to be able to make:

Analyze	Discuss	Interpret
Apply	Evaluate	Organize

Classify	Explain	Paraphrase
Compare	Extrapolate	Predict
Contrast	Formulate	Produce
Deduce	Generalize	Recall
Define	Give examples	Recognize
Demonstrate	Identify	Relate
Design	Infer	Summarize
Develop	Interpolate	Transfer
Differentiate	Illustrate	Translate

With respect to history or any other subject, behaviorists are by no means in complete agreement about *what* the student should be able to explain or recall or analyze, etc. There are, in other words, differences of opinion about the particular material that should be taught as a means of contributing toward the production of good citizens.

Some would allow the individual teacher a great deal of leeway in this matter, expecting that in making her decision she would take into account the policies of her particular school administration, the recommendations of subject matter experts and of specialists in curriculum construction, the interests and needs of her particular students, the kind of community in which her school is located, and perhaps a number of other factors. Other behaviorists would prefer syllabi that would be used on a statewide or even the federal level, at least on a citywide or district-wide level, spelling out in great detail the specific outcomes that individual teachers would be expected to produce. Some such syllabus would seem to be a practical necessity in any system of accountability with achievement test questions based directly on the stated behavioral objectives. In any case, the important thing to the behaviorist is that whatever is taught, for whatever reason, and regardless of who makes the decision, teachers have a very clear notion of what their students will be able to do as a consequence of their instruction. As might be expected, this notion of trying to reduce complex, cognitive learning to the level of observable behavior does not set well with the humanists.

METHODS OF TEACHING

Behavioral educators do not claim that they know, in exact detail, precisely what the best way is to teach each and every particular subject or skill. They do claim, however, to have at least a few general principles of methodology which they believe can make the educational process considerably more efficient than it has been or would be if carried on in accordance with the romantic assumptions of humanistic psychology.

From the standpoint of behaviorism, every classroom should be not only a place for instruction, but a miniature learning laboratory in which there is ongoing research and experimentation to find or develop more effective methods and materials of instruction. In the terminology of the laboratory, the students' behavior is the dependent variable, the teacher's the independent variable. In attempting to improve the teaching-learning process, behaviorists maintain that one must have a clear understanding of the nature of these two kinds of variables.

There are two main kinds of student behavior: "desired" responses, which the teacher is expected to produce or maintain, and "undesired" responses, which she should extinguish or at least reduce. The latter are commonly referred to as "deviant" or "interfering" behaviors because they inhibit or preclude desired behavior. The desired behaviors, of course, constitute the teacher's objectives.

There are also two main kinds of teacher behavior corresponding to the two main aspects of the teaching process. The first has to do with eliciting the desired responses from the student or eliminating his undesired responses (errors, misconceptions, bad habits, etc.). This is largely a matter of selecting, organizing, preparing and presenting material, of planning lessons, explaining, showing, asking questions, and doing the other kinds of things that are ordinarily implied by the word *teaching* as it is commonly used. This part of the teacher's job might be referred to as programming.

The second aspect of teaching is no less important than the first, but is frequently neglected and ordinarily is not thought of as part of the teaching process at all. Here we are referring to reinforcement. This type of teacher behavior involves responding in some way to what the student says or does. Reinforcement has to do with encouraging the student, providing him with feedback to let him know how he's doing, and rewarding him periodically to keep him going. The reward, of course, need not be a gold medal or a bag of gumdrops, but should at least take the form of a word or sign of approval or support. Simply telling the student regularly that he's right or doing fine might be enough. As part of the reinforcement process, errors or misunderstandings or misbehavior may have to be corrected, but the behaviorist maintains that if the teacher has done a good job of programming, such undesired responses will be few and far between.

PROGRAMMING

Once she has selected, refined, and carefully stated her objectives, the behavioristic teacher's next task is to plan her strategies, that is, to decide on the most effective way of bringing about the desired responses on the part of her pupils. This, of course, involves devising or selecting methods and materials that are likely to be most productive for that particular purpose in that particular classroom. She may consult with her students in deciding what they should learn and how they should learn it. But in the final analysis, it is her responsibility to plan, organize, and direct the work of the class in such a way that they do learn it.

The behavioristic teacher can use just about any methodology that she knows of. She can work with individual students on a one to one basis, with small subgroups, or with the class as a whole. She can lecture, explain, demonstrate, use visual aids, teaching machines, or whatever other equipment might be available. She can conduct discussions, have students give reports, assign independent work, or encourage student initiated projects. She can even arrange the learning situation so that students will learn through what they think are their own discoveries. In connection with any of these procedures, however, she is likely to make use of some form of programming.

In programming, the material to be learned is broken down into small segments. The subject (e.g. American History) is broken down into units (e.g. the American Revolution), the units into subunits (e.g. the Declaration of Independence) and the subunits into concepts or even smaller components (e.g. who wrote it, what it stated, when and where it was signed). These segments are presented to the student systematically in small, sequential steps. The student is expected to respond to each of these presentations by doing or saying something to indicate that he has learned them. Ideally, each of his responses is immediately reinforced.

In programming, the material is organized and presented in such a way—bit by bit, step by step, with ample cues, frequent reinforcement, and a great deal of review—that the student is almost certain to respond in the desired way. With this system of feedback and encouragement and with this almost constant direction, the student masters one fact or concept or principle or whatever before proceeding to the next. In this way, mastery of each segment and eventually mastery of the whole unit or subject is supposed to be assured.

While programming might involve the use of computers or teaching machines or programmed textbooks, it need not. Many behaviorists do not share Skinner's belief that mechanical or electronic devices can be made to program students more efficiently than human teachers can. They are inclined to regard these as potentially useful, but not essential, tools, more useful for some purposes than others. Programming, they insist, is what well-organized, systematic teachers have been doing for centuries, but in a less sophisticated manner, perhaps, than is presently known to be possible. All they are really suggesting, they claim, is that teachers be aware of what effective teaching involves, and that they consciously and deliberately try to teach in a more logical, precise, scientific manner.

As for teacher training, behaviorists insist that young men and women can and should be programmed to program their prospective students more effectively. This is just another way of affirming the great emphasis behaviorists place on methodology, their belief that specific methodology can be taught, and their belief that teachers should be systematically trained to function as efficient behavioral engineers. The recent interest in Competency Based Teacher Education (CBTE) is very much in line with this position. CBTE, as it is fondly called by its proponents, is not so much a specific proposal as it is an idea that teacher certification should be based on demonstrated skills rather than an accumulation of college credits. While such programs have been instituted in some colleges or departments of education and are being considered in many others, one of the problems has been that of identifying the particular "competencies" that a teacher needs in order to do her job well. Humanists, as we might expect, are no more enthusiastic about the programming of teachers than they are about the programming of students.

TEACHING MACHINES

In addition to the loose way in which they state their objectives and their inability or unwillingness to program their students, a major reason why many teachers are ineffective, according to B. F. Skinner, is that they do not, and often cannot, give their students sufficient positive reinforcement. At this point we should recall the basic premise of operant conditioning that behavior is shaped by its consequences, that people learn to act in ways that have somehow been rewarded or followed by pleasant effects. Traditionally, schools have relied for this purpose on such incentives as high test grades, good report card marks, gold stars, honor rolls, and deans' lists. Since these rewards are based, for the most part, on competition, they are given only to a relatively few of the best students. Most pupils in a typical classroom, according to Skinner, receive very little reinforcement at all. *only the best get it.*

Ideally, at every step of the learning sequence, particularly in the early stages, every response of every student would be regularly and immediately reinforced. It is mainly because of the inability of a human teacher to provide all this reinforcement that Skinner recommends the use of machines. The machine does not and need not, of course, dispense a food pellet every time a student gives a correct answer. But in a subtle yet effective way it does let him know that his answer is correct and is supposed to reward him with a feeling of accomplishment. It's almost as though his human teacher kept telling him: "That's right ... that's good ... you're doing fine ... keep up the good work."

Although teaching machines have not as yet proved to be as successful as some people expected they would be, their proponents persist in maintaining that they have a tremendous potential and are only in need of technical refinement. The proponents of educational technology claim that the machine can not only provide the necessary continuous reinforcement automatically, but that it can also contribute significantly to the individualization and overall improvement of instruction.

With material that is deemed necessary for all students to learn, machines enable each to proceed at his own rate. Some might master the assigned material in a matter of days; others might need weeks or even months to get through the same program. But everyone, according to the technologists, will learn the prescribed material without the threat or fear of failure, and will learn it thoroughly. Different kinds of programs, moreover, can be designed for different students taking into account their particular abilities, interests, etc. Furthermore, it is claimed, the machine frees the teacher from much of the routine activity that her job entails—reviewing, drilling, repeating, etc., and allows her more time to work with individuals on more creative types of learning experiences.

INDIVIDUALLY PRESCRIBED INSTRUCTION

No less than their humanistic counterparts, behavioral educators are very much concerned with the problem of individualizing instruction. To a behaviorist, however, individualization does not mean letting each student do what he feels like doing. It means teaching him the subject matter and skills that the school administration thinks he should learn and that his parents want him to learn, but in a manner based on his particular abilities, needs, and style of learning. Behaviorists, as we have seen, believe that technology has a great deal to offer in this respect. They recommend not only teaching machines and programmed textbooks, but also films and film strips, records and tapes, closed circuit television, computer-assisted instruction programs, and whatever other mechanical or electronic devices might be available, to be used by students on an individual basis. Apart from technology, they are disposed to look with favor on something like Individually Prescribed Instruction programs which they refer to affectionately as IPI. The way IPI usually works is somewhat as follows.

Early in the term, each student is given a diagnostic pre-test to find out what he already knows about or what he can do in such basic subjects as reading, arithmetic, spelling, and science. On the basis of the pre-test results, the teacher writes out a prescription for each student, somewhat as a physician might do, in terms of his individual weaknesses or needs. What the teacher's prescription amounts to is an individual lesson plan for each student, specifying his objectives for that day. The student is provided with specially prepared worksheets geared to his specific objectives and other self-instructing material as needed so that he can work independently without reference to what any of his fellow students might be doing. They have their own prescriptions. Thus, while one little fellow might be learning to subtract one two-digit number from another two-digit number without "borrowing," the guy next to him might be subtracting three-digit numbers of a magnitude that do require borrowing.

The prescribed objectives are stated in such a way that

they can usually be achieved in one day. The following day the students' workbook is checked or he is given a test to ascertain how well he has achieved them. His particular errors and difficulties are noted and he is given whatever special help he might need. He remains with his first prescription until he achieves "mastery," which usually means 85 percent success with the designated task.

Having achieved the specified level of achievement with his first prescription, he is now ready to go on to the next. The prescriptions are sequentially arranged from the relatively simple to the progressively more complex. Thus, the student takes one small forward step at a time and receives daily feedback, but is not permitted to go on to more advanced work until he has demonstrated his mastery of the necessary prerequisites. The basic strategy of IPI, you will recognize, is essentially the same programmatic procedure used in teaching machines.

When IPI is used, the teacher does very little lecturing to the whole group. The biggest part of her job is helping individuals, preparing the daily prescriptions, diagnosing students' needs, and evaluating their performance. Because of the large amount of testing and record keeping that the system calls for and because of the practical housekeeping problems involved in organizing the necessary materials, to say nothing of the demands on the teacher's time for individual assistance, IPI almost demands the use of teacher aides. Commercially prepared IPI packets are available, but some ambitious, creative teachers prefer to devise their own for use on an occasional, rather than a regular basis. As is so often the case with "new" methods and techniques, some teachers who have used IPI are enthused about it. Others have failed to see that it has worked any wonders. Some feel that it's more bother than it's worth.

TOKEN REINFORCEMENT

As part of the behavioristic revival of the late 1960s and early 1970s, a number of educators and psychologists have been experimenting with more tangible reinforcers than what machines have had to offer. Among these tangible reinforcers are the little plastic chips or slips of paper called tokens which are given to children for specified behavior. When enough are accumulated they can be exchanged for candy, toys, comic books, a bottle of pop, a bag of potato chips, a trip to the zoo or museum or movies, a transistor radio, a specified amount of free time, or whatever else the teacher can and wants to offer.

Unlike the traditional incentives, tokens are not awarded on the basis of competition; every child who acts in the desired way can expect to be rewarded. The terms of the implicit (or maybe explicit) contract are such that every student who gets, say, 80 percent on an arithmetic test or 100 percent on a spelling test receives a certain number of tokens. The agreement might be such that every student who does his homework, or arrives at school on time, or who remains quietly in his seat for a specified length of time, or does whatever else it might be that the teacher wants him to do is similarly rewarded.

This practice has been criticized on the grounds that it rewards people for doing what they should be doing "voluntarily," without getting paid for it. Behaviorists agree that it would be nice if students learned what they were expected to learn simply because it was expected of them. Life in the classroom would be beautiful if students worked because of "intrinsic motivation" or some inborn tendency toward scholastic achievement, but our behavioristic friends don't see that things work that way. If the satisfactions or consequences of "goofing off" are greater or more pleasant than those of studying algebra, the student will inevitably goof off. Assuming that the learning of algebra is all that important, these friends wonder what's so bad about giving students something tangible as a reward for doing so.

The token system, and the giving of cash instead of mere tokens, has been found to be quite effective in a number of schools throughout the country. Particularly in mental institutions and in work with delinquents and retarded children, it seems to have worked when nothing else did. Thus far it seems to be the most effective of the many innovations and experiments tried with so-called disadvantaged children. Apparently many of those who are not turned on by the desire for good grades and are unconcerned about the possibility of academic failure have done what was expected of them because of the tangible reward involved.

Critics of the token system, and of the principle of reinforcement in general, have referred to it as a form of bribery. Behaviorists feel that the use of the term *bribery* is not quite fair since it denotes paying someone secretly for doing something illegal. There is, of course, nothing illegal about the teaching of algebra and the tokens, where used at all, are not given out secretly. Some behavioral engineers suggest that in this respect as in many others, education has a lesson to learn from business and industry: if having people do something is really important, whether it be tightening bolts on an assembly line, teaching kids how to read, or learning to read oneself, it may be necessary to pay them for doing so. To most behaviorists, though, the use of tokens or the awarding of money is no more essential than the use of computers in the educational process. Both are helpful, but neither is considered absolutely necessary.

CLASSROOM MANAGEMENT

Let's relate some of the principles of behavior modification which we have been considering to the problem of classroom management or, as a behaviorist might prefer to call it, classroom control. To begin with, behavioristic educators are not bound by romantic notions of the child's "natural goodness" and are unlikely to regard rules and regulations over student behavior as infringements on their personal autonomy. They have no doubts about the child's need for discipline or about their own responsibility for changing and controlling students' behavior.

Behaviorists, you will recall, explain disruptive, interfering behavior as they do any other form of behavior, in terms of operant conditioning. They hold that children (and adults) misbehave because they have learned to do so, because they have been reinforced for acting in that particular manner. Although the exact nature of the reinforcer might not be apparent, chances are that in a great many cases it is the attention of the teacher or classmates. Simply being noticed can be one of the most powerful of all reinforcers.

Teachers and parents sometimes make the mistake of reinforcing the very behavior they want to extinguish, while ignoring (nonreinforcing) the behavior they would like to maintain. Consider, by way of illustration, a classroom of thirty students. Twenty-nine of them are busily engaged in doing their assigned work (desired behavior) while one of them is throwing spitballs. There's no need to tell you which of the thirty gets the lion's share of the teacher's attention.

"Sidney! Stop that! Sidney! Did you hear what I said? Sidney! How many times do I have to tell you? Sidney! I'm not going to speak to you again."

But, of course, she does. Sidney is getting exactly what he wants as the teacher plays directly into his hands. He is in effect being encouraged to continue this form of deviant behavior, is rewarded for doing so, and is learning that throwing spitballs is one way to keep from being a nonentity. If he stops throwing spitballs and settles down to work, he soon finds that, like the other twenty-nine, he is then ignored.

So what does the behaviorist suggest that the teacher do about Sidney? Well, there are a number of possible courses of action. One would be for the teacher to simply ignore his deviant behavior if it is not disrupting the class. There is at least a possibility that if Sidney does not get his teacher's attention, he will eventually tire of his fruitless spitball throwing and stop doing so without being told. Another possibility would be to give Sidney the attention he is seeking but to a greater degree and in a manner different from that which he expects. The teacher could, for example, invite him to the front of the room "where everyone can see how clever you are" and insist that he demonstrate his proficiency in throwing spitballs for, say, five minutes or so.

Other possibilities might be to assign Sidney some productive task which is incompatible with spitball throwing and compliment him upon the completion of that task; or to congratulate the rest of the class for working so quietly; or to offer the students who are working satisfactorily some sort of reward, such as a few minutes free time; or to wait until the precise moment when Sidney is between spitballs and *then* notice him; or to remind Sidney that there are more mature ways of gaining attention that are available to him; or to reinforce him vicariously by reminding him of his good behavior last week or whenever. Among the other possibilities are some form of punishment or negative reinforcement.

PUNISHMENT

Behaviorists do not always agree with one another on the matter of punishment. Some maintain that children should never be punished because punishment is not only ineffective but is likely to do more harm than good. Some recommend punishment only as a last resort after all else has failed. Some not only have no objection to punishment, but regard it as an essential tool in behavior modification. One's position with respect to punishment depends, of course, on what he means by punishment. The term is usually defined as the imposition of a penalty in retaliation for an offense, or the inflicting of pain or deprivation as a retribution for misconduct. One of the essential elements in the concept of punishment, then, would seem to be that of retaliation or retribution or revenge. It is this element of revenge that many educators and psychologists find most objectionable.

Keeping a child after school, or slapping him, or assigning him additional work, or depriving him of some privilege might be effective means of extinguishing one particular form of deviant behavior; and then again, they might not. If they bring about the desired behavior change without also producing concomitant undesired changes in the child's behavior, their use can be justified. But even if the child who is punished for, say, throwing spitballs does not do so again in the immediate future, there is no assurance that thereafter he will always behave as his teacher would like. Indeed, as a means of getting even with the teacher who punished him, he could end up doing something a lot worse than throwing spitballs. The line between punishment and negative reinforcement is so fine that some observers can't see it at all. One difference as I see it is that while both involve unpleasant consequences, in negative reinforcement there is no element of retaliation, no personal animosity, no desire to hurt another person as a means of evening the score. Another difference is that punishment might teach a person to *refrain from* a particular act in order to avoid unpleasant consequences, while negative reinforcement teaches him to *perform* a particular act in order to avoid unpleasant consequences. In other words, punishment corresponds to the elimination of specific undesired behaviors; negative reinforcement corresponds to the production of desired behaviors.

Negative reinforcement as a means of classroom management might consist in arranging conditions so a student can terminate an unpleasant situation immediately by acting in the specific desired way. Our spitball artist, for example, could be made to stand in a corner until he is ready to settle down and do his work. As soon as he indicates his willingness to do so, he is permitted to return to his seat. More commonly, negative reinforcement is used to induce a person to act in the desired way in order to avoid some sort of pain or deprivation or inconvenience in the future. It carries with it, then, at least an implicit threat of punishment, minus the element of revenge.

Behavior modificationists recognize that negative reinforcement (or what we referred to in the last chapter as "aversive control") does have its place. They also recognize that, to be effective, the threat of punishment may have to be carried

132

out. They recognize, moreover, that in certain situations speedy punishment might be the most efficient way of eliminating particular undesired responses. They are, however, inclined to assign top priority not to the extinction of deviant behavior, but to positive reinforcement of desired behavior. Classroom management, to a behaviorist, is essentially a special form of teaching. Like other forms of teaching, it requires a clear set of behavioral objectives and systematic programming in order to attain them.

TEACHING FOR THINKING

Just about everyone, I suppose, would agree that our schools ought to be concerned with developing students' abilities to think clearly, logically, independently, and productively. Many educators, in fact, would not hesitate to assign top priority to the challenging task of helping students learn how to solve problems, reach their own conclusions, formulate and be able to defend their own opinions, make their own decisions, and to think critically and creatively and responsibly. But can such "good thinking" be taught? From the behavioristic standpoint, the answer is yes and no. It depends on what you mean by thinking. Thinking cannot be taught as a whole, all at once, any more than history or science or football or bookkeeping can be. It is much too complex a process. The process can, however, be reduced to small components or particular skills which can be taught.

The first step in the production of good thinkers is the formulation and clarification of appropriate behavioral objectives. This, as we have noted, involves an analysis of the thinking processes, an identification of the particular behaviors that constitute good thinking, a description of what good thinkers do, and a clear conception of what the student should be able to do as a consequence of his instruction in this area.

A good thinker, for example, is able to identify problems;

gather and organize information necessary for the solution of problems; distinguish fact from opinion; draw inferences; weigh evidence; identify assumptions and implications; make comparisons; apply principles to particular situations; evaluate objects and propositions; analyze propaganda; avoid logical fallacies in his own thinking and recognize them in the thinking of others; analyze and synthesize, and interpolate and extrapolate data.

According to behavioristic psychology, skills such as these which constitute, or at least contribute to , effective thinking can be taught much as other skills are taught. Having decided that her students should be able to draw inferences, for example, the teacher can provide them with an incentive for doing so; give them a model or some examples of inferential thinking so they will have a clear idea of what they are expected to do; show them how inferences can be drawn legitimately; explain and demonstrate some illegitimate ways of trying to draw inferences; give them an opportunity, or require them, to practice drawing inferences, beginning with simple and progressing to more complex data; call their errors to their attention; make suggestions for improvement; and continuously provide them with feedback and encouragement. The behavioristic method of teaching thinking, in short, is essentially no different from that of teaching a person how to play bridge or tennis or any other art or skill.

AFFECTIVE EDUCATION

Behavioristic educators are not less concerned than their humanistic colleagues with affective education: that is, with the student's feelings, beliefs, attitudes, values, likes and dislikes, his self-concept, character, and mental health. But in such areas as counseling, moral or social education, and education for personality adjustment, behaviorists favor a much more direct approach than the humanists, as we would expect. According to the behaviorists, the process of affective education involves the specification of objectives or desired responses and a systematic effort to bring about the desired behaviors on the part of the student. In this respect, it is basically the same as cognitive education.

The behaviorist, we must remember, believes that all behavior, including a person's internal behavior, is acquired. His preferences and prejudices, his self-concept, his fears and anxieties, his feelings of inferiority and guilt and hostility, his moral principles and standards, his values and attitudes, his obsessions and feelings of depression, his interests and goals, his perceptions of other people—all of these are learned responses. If they are unsatisfactory, they can be unlearned, through some form of counterconditioning, and better or more "adaptive" responses can be learned in their place.

According to the behaviorists, better affective responses can not only be learned. They can be taught. Thus, the main function of a counselor or a teacher in this regard or a parent or a friend is not simply to "understand" an individual with a personal problem or to "accept" him as he is, but to change his behavior, to teach him to act (internally or externally) in a new and better way. More specifically, the function might be to teach him to eliminate hostile, antisocial behavior and substitute social, nonhostile behavior; or to eliminate shy, withdrawn behavior and to produce outgoing, moderately extroverted behavior; or to change his negative feelings about himself to positive feelings of self-confidence and personal worth; or, perhaps, to change his negative attitudes toward Shakespeare or police officers or algebra or God or Negroes or spinach or education to more positive attitudes.

Remember, the behavioristic assumption that if we want people to act honestly; to detest greed and violence and injustice and selfishness; to respect themselves and the dignity of their fellow man; to comply with legitimate authority and respect the personal and property rights of others; to accept and carry out social responsibilities; to cooperate with one another; to be compassionate toward those in need; to act, in short, as "good citizens"; if we want people to behave in these ways, we must systematically teach them to do so.

6

Humanism
and Behaviorism
Putting It All Together

In the preceding chapters, we have considered what *the* behaviorists and *the* humanists think about education. We have examined some of their assumptions, their criticisms of the schools, and their recommendations for educational reform. But, as has been pointed out, it might be misleading to speak of *the* humanistic or behavioristic positions simply because all of the individuals who might be properly classified as members of one or another of these two schools of thought do not always see eye to eye with one another on every particular point. So we do not really have two entirely homogeneous groups, nor is there one set of views to which all humanists or all behaviorists must subscribe in order to maintain their party membership.

I've used the expression "party membership" because an analogy with political parties might be helpful. Just as there are differences of opinion, or differences of emphasis, within the Democratic and Republican parties, so are there differences within the behavioristic and humanistic camps. While some Democrats, for example, are quite liberal in their social views, others are so conservative as to be practically indistinguishable from certain liberal Republicans. Within each party there is room for a broad range of positions on particular issues and a wide divergence of political philosophies. But presumably all (or most) Democrats (or Republicans) have something in common which unites them and enables us to speak about the two-party system. The same is true of the two psychological systems with which we are dealing. Quite frankly, I would be hard pressed to specify what it is that distinguishes Democrats from Republicans, or to identify the "something" held in common by a majority of individuals in either political party. But I think I can identify some generally accepted concepts, principles, assumptions, and recommendations that characterize humanistic and behavioristic education and set each apart from the other. I think you can, too. Let's see.

Mark a *B* or an *H* in front of each of the following items to indicate whether it applies more closely to behaviorism or humanism.

B The need to regulate or restrict student freedom
H The need for more student freedom

B Teacher-centered classrooms
H Student-centered classrooms

B Authoritarian classroom management
H Democratic classroom management

B Emphasis on external (environmental) factors
H Emphasis on internal factors (e.g. personal autonomy)

B Specific educational objectives
H Broad, general objectives

B Teaching of subject matter
H Teaching of children

B Transmission of predetermined knowledge and skills
H Promotion of each student's individuality

B Programming
H Discovery methods

B Passing on the cultural heritage
H Fostering self-actualization

B Emphasis on the products of learning
H Emphasis on the processes of learning

B Giving the correct answer
H Learning how to learn

B Logical organization of material
H Psychological organization

B Carefully prepared lesson plans
H Flexibility and adaptability

B Systematic methodology
H Spontaneity and improvisation

B Formal instruction
H Informal instruction

B Expository teaching
H Student activity

B Teacher accountability
H Student responsibility

B Emphasis on efficiency in teaching
H Emphasis on enjoyment in learning

B Desired response
H Meaning and relevance

B *Walden Two* as a kind of ideal
H Summerhill as a kind of ideal

B Teaching as a science
H Teaching as an art

B Teacher regarded as a technician or engineer
H Teacher regarded as a facilitator

B Drill, repetition, and review for mastery
H More variety than repetition

B Objective tests
H Subjective tests

B Wide use of incentives
H More reliance on interest

B Extrinsic motivation
H Intrinsic motivation

B Based on scientific realism or positivism
H Based on phenomenology or relativism

B Computer assisted instruction
H Emphasis on creativity and self-expression

B Criticized for being mechanistic, deterministic
H Criticized for being romantic, overly idealistic

140

B Emphasis on reinforcement
H Emphasis on goal-seeking

B Directive counseling
H Nondirective counseling

B Aims at producing the good citizen
H Aims at producing the free and happy person

B Performance contracts
H Open classrooms

In each of the sets, as I'm sure you've recognized, the first item pertains to behaviorism, the second to humanism.

FORMULATING YOUR OWN SYSTEM

Having sorted the above concepts into two bags, you are now in a position to decide which, if either, you want to buy. Perhaps, like me, you aren't ready to buy either package as a whole. I can think of no good reason why you should. Perhaps you'd prefer to shop selectively, *a la carte* as it were, and put together your own personal "do it yourself" system of educational psychology, selecting what you regard as the best items from both the humanistic and behavioristic groupings.

If you begin with the need for more student freedom, for example, there's no law that says you have to take the student-centered classroom concept along with it. If you are favorably disposed toward the student-centered classroom, you need not accept the Summerhill version or even the open classroom. If you choose the teacher-centered classroom, you will probably also choose "carefully prepared lesson plans" as well, but you certainly need not accept computer assisted instruction or "drill, repetition, and review." Even with the logical organization and systematic methodology of a teacher-centered classroom, you need not reject the flexibility and adaptability, the spontaneity and improvisation that are more closely associated with the student-centered classroom.

In formulating your own personal theory of instruction you will want to put together a set of principles that are logically consistent and psychologically sound. In doing so you should not be hampered by what appear to be dichotomies between such concepts as freedom and control, authoritarian and democratic management, student-centered and teacher-centered classrooms. These are not pairs of mutually exclusive, separate and distinct ideas; they represent, rather, terminal, and maybe even extreme, positions on a kind of continuum. Perhaps you are unwilling to accept either of what you regard as extremes. Having emphasized the differences between humanism and behaviorism in the preceding chapters, I do not now wish to minimize them. But I should like to suggest some ways whereby some of the practical educational implications of these two systems might be harmonized.

THE ROLE OF THE SCHOOL

Both humanism and behaviorism support the overriding importance of education as a means of helping to solve the kinds of problems we noted at the very beginning of Chapter 1. Both, moreover, accept the distinction we made early in that chapter between education and schooling. Both perceive the school as only one of many educational agencies, and both recognize that without the cooperation of others, especially the family, the school will be severely limited with respect to what it can accomplish.

There is no official humanistic or behavioristic position on compulsory school attendance or the question of alternatives to existing schools. Because of the emphasis they place on man's capacity for and right to self-determination and their preference for informality in education, the humanists are likely to be more favorably disposed to the prospects of alternatives, but the behaviorists are by no means committed to the preservation of our existing system of compulsory school attendance. Both behaviorists and humanists would rather have schools so attractive that students would want to attend them, than laws requiring them to do so.

The point on which they are more likely to differ concerns the purpose of the school, the purpose of education, and the relationship between the two. If forced to summarize the purpose of education in a few words, humanists, as we have seen, might well respond in terms of self-actualization, and behaviorists in terms of transmission of the cultural heritage. But a moderate from either camp might well suggest that the acquisition of certain intellectual skills, bodies of knowledge, values and beliefs, is an indispensable condition for self-actualization. He might maintain, and you might agree, that in a broad sense self-actualization can properly be considered the purpose of education, while the purpose of the schools is to help the individual actualize himself by teaching him those things he needs which he could not learn as well informally outside the school. A number of questions would still remain, however, about what those things are, how they should be taught, and who should decide.

TEACHER OR STUDENT-CENTERED CLASSROOMS

Perhaps you are inclined to agree with the humanists that classroom activities should be based on the existing interests, needs, and purposes of the students. But perhaps you also think that there are certain things that everyone in a particular class should be expected to learn whether or not he happens to be particularly interested in them or sees the immediate need for learning them. At the elementary school level, you might regard the three R's as examples of these "certain things." At the high school level you might favor an extremely liberal elective system, but after a student freely chooses a particular subject, you might want to hold him accountable for mastering the content of that subject.

Perhaps you think there are ways to help each student learn the essentials in his own way and at his own rate and maybe in varying degrees, depending on his particular abilities, background, and other individual factors. Perhaps you think that a big part of a teacher's job is to find and use such ways and means. Maybe you like the idea of teaching children rather than subject matter, or maybe you prefer the reverse. But I'm confident that you are perceptive enough to think in terms of teaching children *something,* or of teaching subject matter *to someone.*

Perhaps you believe that students should actively participate in planning their school programs, formulating their objectives, working out their methodologies, and evaluating their own work. But perhaps you also think the teacher should have the final word in matters such as these.

Perhaps you think the school should be concerned with preparing the child for the future but should also recognize that he is living in the here and now, where he has needs which the school can help satisfy. While you might feel that transmission of certain predetermined aspects of the cultural heritage is one purpose, and perhaps the main single purpose, of the school, you might agree that the school has other purposes as well. Among these other purposes you might want to include the development in the student of a sense of responsibility, particularly for his own education. You might also want to include such purposes as the development of his initiative, creativity, self-confidence, decision-making abilities, and powers of self-expression.

For purposes such as these, you might favor considerably more in the way of student centeredness than is likely to be found in the conventional school. But perhaps you would want to draw the line at having the student alone be completely responsible for making the many decisions involved in his educational program.

Seeing some pros and cons in each, some advantages and disadvantages to both, perhaps you are unwilling to accept either a completely teacher-centered or student-centered classroom. As I suggested earlier, there is no good reason why you should. Maybe you have already concluded that the only position that really makes sense is a combination of the two: a system that is dominated by neither the teacher nor the student, but is intelligently and cooperatively governed by both.

Maybe as a teacher you would like to lean as far as possible in the direction of student centeredness without losing your balance, believing that you have a responsibility to each student to help him learn as much as possible of what society expects him to learn in the most effective way possible, and that this is a responsibility you really cannot abdicate or delegate.

THE "GOOD" TEACHER

In formulating a theoretical framework of education on which to base your practice, you can hardly avoid the question, what is or what makes a good teacher? Your answer, of course, will depend on what you mean by the word *good* in this context. Behaviorists and humanists, like everyone else, are in agreement on the need for good teachers. But they approach the problem of defining and identifying good teachers from two rather different viewpoints. Humanists are particularly interested in the *teacher as a person*, while behaviorists are more concerned with the *person as a teacher*. There are some real differences here, at least in emphasis, but let's see whether you can resolve them to your own satisfaction.

Humanists, you will recall, do not think that teachers can be adequately evaluated on the basis of their methodology alone. They maintain that teaching is not a routine mechanical process but essentially a personal encounter between a unique, individual teacher and unique, individual students. They believe that all good teachers do not act in the same way or possess the same characteristics or use the same techniques. For reasons such as these, they believe that there is no one best method of teaching, no formula to ensure teacher effectiveness, no objective way of evaluating teachers. Humanists, then, are inclined to stress the teacher's personality above her behavior. It's not what the teacher does, they are fond of saying, but the kind of person she is that makes the difference. The good teacher, they maintain, is first and foremost a warm, friendly, sympathetic, understanding, sensitive human being who loves her students and has a genuine desire to help them

Behaviorists have nothing against teachers who are warm, kind, and friendly. They certainly do not recommend that teachers be cold, hostile, insensitive robots who hate kids or want to harm them. But they maintain that warmth, kindness, friendliness, and good intentions are not nearly enough to teach a child how to read or spell or add fractions or play basketball. Certain skills or competencies or "know how" are required, and these are likely to be of far greater consequence than the teacher's degree of warmth or friendliness, which, incidentally, are nothing more than one person's subjective impressions of another. Humanists, in turn, have nothing against skills or competencies or techniques, but insist that these alone which, incidentally, can be programmed into a machine, do not constitute a good teacher either.

Perhaps you find the humanistic ideal a fine model for the personality of a teacher or, for that matter, of any other human being. Maybe you feel that it would be nice if everybody were friendly, sympathetic, and warmhearted. Maybe you think that because of the very nature of her job it is especially important for a teacher, even more so than those engaged in most other occupations or professions, to be generous, considerate, accepting, etc. Perhaps you believe that in the very important area of human relationships between teacher and students and with regard to such matters as the teacher's attitude toward her students, you would want to be guided by this humanistic ideal.

But perhaps you would also agree that when it comes to the day-to-day work of a teacher: planning lessons, formulating objectives, preparing materials, organizing student activities, leading discussions, asking questions, explaining and demonstrating new material, identifying students' strengths and weaknesses, diagnosing and correcting their errors, providing extra help to those who may need it, managing the behavior of some thirty healthy, active youngsters, trying to preserve a degree of sanity in the classroom, satisfying administrative requirements with respect to record keeping, form filling, report card marking, etc.—something more than love is needed. Perhaps at this down-to-earth level, you think the behaviorists might have a point.

Perhaps you have strong reservations about the concept of accountability and the behaviorists' mechanical model of efficient, effective teaching. Perhaps you are somewhat less than enthusiastic about the idea of a teacher being a behavioral engineer and perhaps the whole behavioristic approach to the question of what constitutes good teachers strikes you as being cold and impersonal. But perhaps the humanistic model impresses you as being somewhat vague and unrealistic, as something less than adequate as a source of practical assistance with the kinds of things we have just noted that teachers are paid to do and that society expects them to do. Perhaps you find that the humanists are right in describing the kind of person a good teacher ought to be, and that the behaviorists are right in focusing on some of the kinds of things that person should be able to do.

THEORY AND METHODOLOGY

Humanists and behaviorists agree that one thing a teacher needs is a theory of learning, or at least a set of principles or assumptions about the learning process, on which to base her methods of teaching. In earlier chapters we considered the humanistic view of learning as essentially a matter of discovery and the behaviorist view as programming or operant conditioning. If you're a bit hazy about these concepts, you might want to review the sections on "Discovery and Personal Meaning" and "Teachers and Their Methods" in Chapter 3, and those on "Methods of Teaching" and "Programming" in Chapter 5.

Perhaps you think that programming would be more effective with some subjects and the discovery method with others. Maybe even within the same subject area, you see some units or lessons with which discovery would seem to be more appropriate and others where you would prefer programming. Perhaps you are favorably disposed toward the informality of a humanistic classroom but also see the need for the kind of structure, organization, advance planning, and follow-through recommended by the behaviorists. Please remember that there is no law of logic or psychology or pedagogy to prevent you from alternating between these two methods, or modifying or combining them as you see fit. I can assure you that neither has been proved superior to the other, in general or in connection with any particular subject. So you may, if you wish, use programming in the morning and discovery in the afternoon. If you do, you will be no more inconsistent than you would be if you used, say, workbooks for some learning experiences and visual aids or panel discussions with others.

Perhaps you would like to use such ideas as behavioral objectives, logical organization, careful lesson planning, and systematic positive reinforcement, but still don't want to think of yourself as a "mere" technician or behavioral engineer. As I suggested earlier, maybe you can alleviate this difficulty simply by substituting some form of the word *teach* whenever you encounter the verbs *program* or *condition.* If you wish, you can even use the expression "facilitate learning" instead of teach.

As a teacher, you might want to transmit part of the cultural heritage (or teach subject matter), but not by programming techniques. Perhaps you would prefer to use some form of the discovery method in order to help your students derive personal meaning from, and perceive the relevance of, your material. If you do so, you can think of yourself as using humanistic means to achieve behavioristic ends. Perhaps in other situations you may find yourself using behavioristic means to achieve humanistic goals by, for example, programming your students to develop self-confidence or a feeling of personal worth.

You might find the discovery approach particularly helpful in introducing a new unit of work. By inviting your students to ask questions, express their opinions, and see what they can find out about the new topic on their own, perhaps you can not only stimulate interest but also save yourself a lot of unnecessary explaining. Maybe, in the best humanistic, student-centered tradition, you can enlist their assistance in formulating objectives and deciding on procedures. Then, if you wish, you can begin programming. But perhaps you will find that they are doing so well that programming is unnecessary.

Programming, of course, is not simply or even mainly a matter of explaining or presenting material. One of the most effective means of programming consists of asking the right questions in the right sequence and thus "drawing out" the student. In this way, you might be able to arrange your classroom activities so that students discover (or think they discover) the predetermined material or behaviors you want them to learn. In some situations, if left to their own devices, your students might soon discover that the most effective and economical way of their learning something that they want to learn is to have you formally teach it to them.

You might also want to consider the possibility of systematically teaching children how to go about the business of independently discovering knowledge or meaning for themselves. Maybe you can program your students to observe and ask questions and experiment and figure things out for themselves more efficiently. This possibility might strike you as being contradictory—programming kids to work independently and creatively. But it might make more sense to you than the idea of "turning the students loose" and expecting them to discover how to discover, or learn how to learn, on their own. If you would like them to do independent library research, for example, you might want them to spend a couple of days trying to discover how to use the card catalogue and find the necessary reference books, and the time might be well spent. But you might prefer to save time and confusion by carefully teaching these things in advance.

Maybe the behavioristic emphasis on "efficiency" in learning does not set very well with you. Maybe it smacks too much of the General Motors way of doing things and impresses you as being somehow dehumanizing. Perhaps the humanistic emphasis on enjoyment of learning appeals to you more. Efficiency, of course, does not preclude enjoyment nor does enjoyment preclude efficiency. More often they tend to support one another. Usually, the more efficiently we are able to perform in a given area, the more we are likely to enjoy the experience, and the more we enjoy an activity, the more effort we are likely to put forth and the more productive we are likely to become.

So if you want to program, then program. If you're the kind, warm friendly, generous, sympathetic, loving kind of person we talked about in the previous section, I doubt that your students would mind having you program them. In fact, they might even enjoy the experience and profit by it. But allow some time for discovery, too.

INDIVIDUALIZATION

Behavioristic, no less than humanistic, educators are very much concerned with the problem of individualizing instruction. This, in fact, is one of the oldest and most difficult problems in all of education. A wide variety of practices and procedures have been tried in an attempt to solve the problem, or at least to help provide for differences among students in their abilities, needs, backgrounds, etc., but thus far none of them has met with overwhelming success. Some of these attempts, such as the open classroom and free schools, are derivatives of humanistic psychology. Others, such as the use of teaching machines and individual prescribed instruction programs, are more in keeping with behaviorism. Still others, such as homogeneous groupings, nongraded classrooms, enrichment programs, acceleration, flexible scheduling, mini-courses, independent study programs, work-study programs, and a number of other "alternatives" are not necessarily tied to either of the two main psychological systems but could be used with either.

Perhaps you are committed to the idea of gearing the instructional program to the interests and abilities and needs of individual students, but are less than enthusiastic about the prospects of allowing each student to decide what, if anything, he is to learn and how and when and to what degree he will attempt to learn it. Perhaps you feel that teaching machines and computers have their place in a classroom along with visual aids, textbooks, and encyclopedias, but you do not see them as answers to the individualization problem either. Perhaps you think that something like individually prescribed instruction is a step in the right direction but you would prefer a strategy that is a bit more humanistic. Perhaps in your attempt to combine what you regard as the most desirable features of humanism and behaviorism you would like to consider some form of contract plan as a means of individualization along with some of the other possibilities that have been mentioned.

Basically, here's how contract plans work: Each student enters into a contractual agreement with his teacher specifying the amount and quality of work he will do in some particular subject area. Each student has his own individual written contract. The terms of the contract are not imposed on him; he and his teacher negotiate them. He may select his project, or task or assignment or whatever it might be called, from a list which the teacher offers, or he may devise one of his own, subject to her approval. This element of giving the student a choice of what he will do brings joy and gladness to the hearts of the humanists. The behaviorists are also elated because the contract does specify, in behavioral terms, what the student will be expected to accomplish. Each student, in effect, has his own individualized set of behavioral objectives which he freely accepts. The contract also specifies the expected standards or criteria that will be used in evaluating the project as well as the reward the student will receive upon the successful completion of his part of the bargain.

Some sort of *quid pro quo* is, of course, a condition of any contract: you give me something and I'll give you something. To the extent that you're behavioristically inclined, the idea of specified-in-advance reinforcers should be appealing. You can, if you wish, use some form of the "token economy" in this context or you can rely on "grades" or some more traditional kind of reinforcer if you and your students agree. Giving the student an opportunity to help decide not only what his task will be but also what his particular reinforcer will be should appeal to your humanistic inclinations.

The contract concept is not offered as a panacea, but it is an instrument that just about any teacher can use in just about any classroom without a drastic overhauling of the entire school system or a vast expenditure of money and without antagonizing humanistic or behavioristic critics very much. Moreover, the plan is flexible enough so that it can be used on a daily, weekly, quarterly, or annual basis and can be adapted for use at any grade level.

There are, as I have suggested, other ways of attempting individualization, but none that I know of that is completely satisfying to every humanist or every behaviorist, much less to every member of both parties. But please remember, especially now that we're on the subject of individualization, that you're under no obligation as a teacher or a prospective teacher or an educational theorist or a human being to even try to satisfy every humanist or every behaviorist or every anyone else. You couldn't, even if you wanted to.

Perhaps in your approach to this problem, in the preplanning stage, you would like to begin with a humanistic concept of what the individual student is and what he is capable of becoming. In planning his program or designing his curriculum and in formulating and carrying out your teaching strategies to help him you might want to be somewhat more behavioristic. In trying to create a kind of classroom climate in which to implement your plans, you might wish to follow the suggestions of the humanists. And when difficulties arise, with the slow learner, for example, and remedial work is necessary, you might want to return to a behavioristic posture.

MOTIVATION

Early in this chapter you were given a little test in which you were asked to indicate whether each of a number of concepts applied more closely to behaviorism or humanism. If you marked a *B* in front of "wide use of incentives," "extrinsic motivation," and "emphasis on reinforcement," and an *H* in front of "more reliance on interest," "intrinsic motivation," and "emphasis on goal seeking," you were right. Those answers would suggest that you have a pretty good basic understanding of the differences between humanistic and behavioral theories of motivation. Still, at this point, you might find it helpful to review the sections on "Goals" in Chapter 2, "Motivation" in Chapter 3, and "Reinforcement" in Chapter 4.

Perhaps you feel that the differences between interests and incentives, intrinsic and extrinsic motivation, and between reinforcement and goal seeking are rather artificial and academic. Perhaps you think these distinctions have some theoretical significance, but believe that at the practical, operational level they have been overemphasized. In trying to understand why people do the things they do and how they are or can be motivated, perhaps you believe that much human behavior is performed because a person has somehow acquired an interest in gaining some sort of external reward (or incentive), the prospects or attainment of which he perceives as internally satisfying.

Consider, for example, such concepts as attention, approval, and esteem. Humanists tell us that these are among man's principal goals. Behaviorists include these as among man's most powerful reinforcers. Perhaps you feel that the satisfaction of these needs or the attainment of these goals constitutes positive reinforcement. Perhaps you recognize the utility of reinforcement from external sources as a means of motivating some people toward some kinds of behavior. But perhaps you also recognize that the highest and most desirable kind of reinforcement is the feeling of satisfaction or accomplishment that comes from within an individual. Perhaps you would consider the individual's perception of the personal meaning of a subject or an activity, or his recognition of its relevance as essentially a form of internal reinforcement.

Perhaps you agree with the humanists that, insofar as possible, classroom activities and learning experiences should be based on the student's existing interests. You might also agree with the behaviorists that interests are not innate, but acquired, and that part of a teacher's job is to develop new interests. Perhaps you believe that the subject you are teaching is so important that students should learn it even though they do not find it interesting in and of itself. Maybe you recognize that no matter what you do, you will not always be able to develop the interest you would like the student to have in that subject. You might then want to rely on some sort of incentive or external reinforcer. Perhaps you will find that the frequent systematic use of such reinforcers is an effective means of arousing and holding the student's attention and of getting him to set forth the effort necessary to learn your subject. At that point you might find your students gradually becoming interested enough in your subject so that you can gradually begin withdrawing your reinforcers.

In attempting to arouse and maintain students' interest and in trying to get them to set forth the necessary effort to learn your subject, you might begin as a humanist by helping them perceive how that subject will help them become what they want to become and are capable of becoming. This, of course, assumes that you yourself have a genuine humanistic interest in each of your students as a fellow human being, and a strong desire to help him develop his particular set of potentialities. If the use of some sort of behavioristic incentive or some form of competition promises to be helpful for this purpose, I see no reason why you should not use it.

I am not suggesting that the theoretical differences between humanists and behaviorists on the motivation problem can be quickly and nicely resolved. And I certainly am not implying that the practical problems of classroom motivation can be easily overcome by using a little of this and a little of that. But I am suggesting that in this area, as in the others we have been considering, you need not think in either-or terms. You can, rather, use and fuse ideas from both of the theories in formulating a framework on which you can base your practice as a teacher.

FREEDOM AND CONTROL

Perhaps you believe that students' freedom should be respected and cultivated but you don't think they should be completely at liberty to do as they please in school or for that matter anywhere else. Perhaps you are convinced that some rules and regulations are not only desirable but essential for the welfare of the individual as well as the good of his society. Maybe you feel that the concept of individual freedom carried to an extreme would result in anarchy, while an exaggerated notion of the individual's need for external control over his behavior could lead to tyranny. I presume that neither anarchy nor tyranny appeals to you, but I'm sure you realize that these are not the only options available.

Maybe you like the connotations of the word democratic better than those of authoritarian, but maybe you also distinguish between authoritarian and autocratic. Maybe you believe that in a classroom the teacher ought to have somewhat more authority than her students and that she can and should use that authority to regulate their behavior without being a tyrant. Perhaps you are inclined toward the humanistic view that most students are basically good and trustworthy. But perhaps you find that they do have tendencies to get out of line once in a while or, as the behaviorists would put it, they learn to misbehave and need some system of control.

The romantic critics, you will recall, claim that many schools and classrooms are characterized by "petty, oppressive rules," imposed at the whims of and for the convenience of teachers and administrators, but having little or nothing to do with education or the development of the child. Behaviorists would certainly agree that if a particular school does indeed have excessive, unreasonable, unnecessary, and inhumane restrictions on students' behavior, those restrictions ought to be abolished as quickly as possible. But they think it would be a mistake to go to the opposite extreme and do away with rules altogether or turn the entire school government over to the kids. Perhaps you would not want your own children brought up in the kind of concentration camp atmosphere the romantics depict and condemn, but then neither would an out-and-out behaviorist. Perhaps you would not want to send your children to Summerhill or to an American free school but neither would a great many humanists.

Perhaps you agree with the humanists that the school should be a pleasant, happy place, but think it should be something more than that. Perhaps you see a distinction between the school as a place for academic learning, and a playground or recreation center as a place primarily devoted to fun and games. But perhaps you feel that even most games really wouldn't be much fun without rules. And I'm sure you realize that even playgrounds and recreation centers need some requirements and prohibitions in order to serve the purpose for which they are intended.

The romantic critics, you will also recall, maintain that our entire system of formal education is based to a very great extent on fear. Behaviorists tend to agree, except that they are more likely to use the term aversive control or negative reinforcement. The behaviorists would much prefer to have education based on what they call positive reinforcement, which implies pleasant consequences. While recognizing the need to extinguish undesirable behavior, they are inclined to place a greater emphasis on the production of desired behaviors. With regard to accentuating the positive, the humanists would certainly agree.

Perhaps your position is that the ideal means of classroom management is to prevent misbehavior from occurring in the first place by arranging conditions so that every student is busily engaged in some interesting task and every student is happy and cooperative because his social and emotional needs are being met. But I'm sure you realize that this is much easier said than done, and that no matter what a teacher does to try to prevent misbehavior, some misbehavior is likely to occur.

Perhaps you think that when a child does misbehave, the friendly, democratic approach that you associate with humanism should be used: talking to the child in a constructive, nonthreatening manner, explaining why he should do this or should not do that, and all the while showing him that you understand him and "accept him as a person," and love him and have a genuine desire to help him. If this approach works, fine. If it does not, perhaps you will want to use some of the principles of behavior modification which were discussed in Chapters 4 and 5.

SUMMARY AND CONCLUSIONS

While humanism and behaviorism offer alternative and often contrasting approaches to the problems of education, throughout this chapter I have been trying to suggest that they are not diametrically opposed to each other on a theoretical level and that from a practical standpoint the implications and applications of each are by no means mutually exclusive. I do not find that behaviorism is necessarily as mechanistic, deterministic, undemocratic, or dehumanizing, as it is sometimes made out to be, nor do I consider humanism to be as unscientific, sentimental, unrealistic, or naively romantic, as its critics claim it is. Surely behaviorism need not imply the mass production of mindless robots any more than humanism necessarily implies a glorification of the "free and noble savage."

To me it seems that our schools can help develop the free and happy, self-actualizing people envisioned by the humanists while at the same time contribute to the development of the good citizens envisioned by the behaviorists. I am convinced, however, that the school alone can provide for all of the educational needs of neither the good citizen nor the free and happy individual. We must think of education in terms considerably broader than schooling.

I feel that neither *the* behaviorists nor *the* humanists have all of the answers to all of the problems of education. But I do believe that between them they have at least some good tentative answers to a great many of those problems and offer some sound direction as to where other answers might be found. What do you think?

Perhaps you are more strongly attracted to one of the two positions than the other, but are unwilling to categorize yourself as an out-and-out humanist or behaviorist. Perhaps you do not like to think of yourself as a dead-center, middle-of-the-roader because you regard middle-of-the-roaders as indecisive or uncommitted or just plain wishy-washy. But perhaps you do see enough merit in the other position so that, for the time being, you would prefer to keep your options open. Maybe you would like to think of yourself as a humanistic behaviorist or a behavioristic humanist. Either of these terms could be used to designate a humanistic person with humanistic attitudes toward students who selectively follow certain behavioristic principles and use behavioral techniques when the time for doing so feels right.

Perhaps you will want to continue to reflect on the implications of these two systems and, as the occasions arise, draw on what you regard as the best of each. Perhaps you will find yourself successfully using humanistic means to achieve behavioral objectives, and behavioral methods to attain humanistic goals.

I'm confident that if you haven't already done so, you will eventually get your thoughts on these matters together and formulate for yourself a theory of education, on which to base your practices, that is neither humanistic nor behavioristic, but yours.

Bibliography

Instead of listing every book on humanism or behaviorism that I have ever heard of, I have selected twenty on each that I can sincerely recommend. I do not suggest that these are necessarily the best books on the subjects, but I do believe that you will get something out of reading, or at least sampling, any or all of them. The books are grouped under two headings, humanism and behaviorism.

HUMANISM

Avila, Donald L. et al., eds. *The Helping Relationship Sourcebook.* Boston: Allyn and Bacon, Inc., 1971. A compilation of short articles from a variety of sources by authors who conceive of teaching and counseling as "helping relationships."

Blitz, Barbara. *The Open Classroom: Making It Work.* Boston: Allyn and Bacon, Inc., 1973. A comprehensive overview of the open classroom concept with many practical suggestions for its implementation at various age levels.

Brown, George I. *Human Teaching for Human Learning.* New York: Viking Press, 1971. A discussion of the human potential movement and some concrete examples of how its methods can be used in classrooms.

Combs, Arthur W. et al. *The Professional Education of Teachers.* 2d ed. Boston: Allyn and Bacon, Inc., 1974. The views of a leading perceptualist on what humanistic teachers are like and how they should be prepared for their professional roles.

Combs, Arthur W. et al. *The Professional Education of Teachers.* 2d ed. Boston: Allyn and Bacon, Inc., 1974. The views of a leading perceptualist on what humanistic teachers are like and how they should be prepared for their professional roles.

Graubard, Allen. *Free the Children: Radical Reform and the Free School Movement.* New York: Pantheon Books, 1973. Summarizes the philosophy underlying Free Schools, describes such schools in operation, and discusses their successes, failures, and prospects for the future.

Holt, John. *Freedom and Beyond.* New York: E. P. Dutton, 1972. The views of one of the best known and most outspoken critics of education on the idea of human freedom as applied to the schools.

Kozol, Jonathon. *Free Schools.* Boston: Houghton Mifflin, 1972. A critical analysis of Free Schools by one of their first and staunchest proponents including his ideas on why so many Free Schools have not lived up to expectations.

Leonard, George. *Education and Ecstasy.* New York: Delacorte Press, 1968. About as romantic as any book and more so than most; this one maintains that education should be an ecstatic experience.

Maslow, Abraham H. *Motivation and Personality.* 2d ed. New York: Harper and Row, 1970. Perhaps the most authoritative book available on self-actualization, this is "a must" for anyone seriously interested in the subject.

_____. *Toward a Psychology of Being.* New York: Van Nostrand, 1962. Written by Mr. Humanistic Psychology, as he has been called, this book is a classic presentation of the principles and assumptions of that system.

Moustakas, Clark, and Perry, Cereta. *Learning to Be Free.* Englewood Cliffs, New Jersey: Prentice Hall, Inc., 1973. The authors' views on how humanistic principles of education can and should be applied in order to help children become active participants in, rather than "victims" of, the educational process.

Neill, A. S. *Summerhill.* New York: Hart Publishing Co., 1970. The late founder and headmaster of this well-known, controversial school describes life at Summerhill and the educational philosophy on which it is based.

Postman, Neil, and Weingartner, Charles. *The School Book.* New York: Delacorte Press, 1973. The authors trace the recent historical development of agitation for school reform and offer their own romantic suggestions for improving the schools.

Rogers, Carl. *Freedom to Learn.* Columbus, Ohio: Charles E. Merrill, 1969. The "father" of client-centered, nondirective psychotherapy explains and illustrates his views on student-centered, nondirective education.

_____. *On Becoming a Person.* Boston: Houghton Mifflin, 1961. In this book, which might be regarded as another classic in the literature of humanistic psychology, one of the founders of Third Force Psychology sets forth his ideas about human nature and the process of becoming what one is capable of becoming.

Silberman, Charles E. *Crisis in the Classroom.* New York: Random House, 1970. One of the most influential books criticizing American education from a romantic point of view and recommending an open classroom approach for its improvement.

Silberman, Melvin E. et al., eds. *The Psychology of Open Teaching and Learning.* Boston: Little, Brown and Co., 1972. A collection of articles written by acknowledged leaders in humanistic education on the psychological theories and principles that underlie an "inquiry approach" to education.

Stanford, Gene, and Roark, Albert. *Human Interaction in Education.* Boston: Allyn and Bacon, Inc., 1974. A detailed explanation of the meaning, implications, and implementation of the idea that education is essentially a social process involving the use of group methods.

Troost, Cornelius J., ed. *Radical School Reform.* Boston: Little, Brown and Co., 1973. This anthology includes articles by a variety of individuals who are critical in one way or another of what they regard as extremism in the romantic-radical school reform movement.

BEHAVIORISM

Ackerman, J. Mark. *Operant Conditioning Techniques for the Classroom Teacher.* Glenview, Illinois: Scott, Foresman and Co., 1972. A short and simple but comprehensive introduction to behavior modification with practical applications to the work of teachers.

Anderson, Richard, and Faust, G. W. *Educational Psychology.* New York: Dodd, Mead and Co., 1973. A partially programmed textbook that explains and exemplifies what the authors call "the science of instruction and learning."

Ayllon, Teodoro, and Azrin, Nathan. *The Token Economy.* New York: Appleton, Century, Crofts, 1968. Explains how behavioral therapy, including token reinforcement, is used in mental hospitals, but the principles discussed have far wider implications.

Baker, Robert L., and Schutz, Richard E., eds. *Instructional Product Development.* New York: Van Nostrand Reinhold Co., 1971. A self-instructing book that introduces the reader to the process of developing programmed instructional materials.

Bandura, Albert. *Principles of Behavior Modification.* New York: Holt, Rinehart and Winston, 1969. The most technical book on this list, recommended for the more advanced reader who is interested in research findings on the subject.

Becker, Wesley C. et al. *Teaching: A Course in Applied Psychology.* Palo Alto, California: Science Research Associates, 1971. An introductory book that explains how behavior modification can be used with problems of motivation, instruction, classroom management, special education, and in "stimulating the intelligent mind."

Becker, Wesley C., ed. *An Empirical Basis for Change in Education.* Palo Alto, California: Science Research Associates, 1971. A book of readings which includes thirty-seven primary-source articles, some rather technical, others more general, on various aspects of behavior modification.

Harris, Mary B., ed. *Classroom Uses of Behavior Modification.* Columbus, Ohio: Charles E. Merrill, 1972. Another anthology of primary source material; includes a helpful introduction, topical index, and concise abstracts of the articles included.

Kibler, Robert J. et al. *Objectives For Instruction and Evaluation.* Boston: Allyn and Bacon, Inc., 1974. Includes numerous examples of, and suggestions for, writing behavioral objectives in the cognitive, affective, and psychomotor domains.

Krumboltz, John D., and Krumboltz, Helen B. *Changing Children's Behavior.* Englewood Cliffs, New Jersey: Prentice-Hall, Inc., 1972. Addressed to parents as well as teachers, this book is organized around thirteen principles of behavior modification with many examples of how each can be used in the home or the classroom.

MacMillan, Donald L. *Behavior Modification in Education.* New York: The Macmillan Co., 1973. Traces the historical development of behavior modification, explains its main principles, applies them to regular and special classrooms, and examines some criticisms and shortcomings of the theory.

Madsen, Charles H., Jr., and Madsen, Clifford K. *Teaching/Discipline: A Positive Approach for Educational Development.* 2d ed. Boston: Allyn and Bacon, Inc., 1974. Analyzes a number of actual situations in which behavioral principles are applied to problems of discipline and classroom management.

Meacham, Merle, and Weisen, Allen E. *Changing Classroom Behavior.* Scranton, Pennsylvania: International Textbook Co., 1969. Subtitled "A Manual for Precision Teaching," this book applies behavioral principles to the education of retarded, socially deprived, and emotionally disturbed children, as well as normal children.

Nagel, Thomas S., and Richman, Paul T. *Competency-Based Instruction.* Columbus, Ohio: Charles E. Merrill Publishing Co., 1972. A short, branching programmed text, this book develops what its subtitle calls "A Strategy to Eliminate Failure."

Pitts, Carl E., ed. *Operant Conditioning in the Classroom.* New York: Thomas Y. Crowell Co., 1971. A book of readings which deal with a diversity of problems from a behavioral point of view.

Skinner, B. F. *Beyond Freedom and Dignity.* New York: Alfred A. Knopf, Inc., 1971. One of the most controversial books in all psychology, in which this leading behaviorist rejects the concepts of freedom and human dignity and calls for a "technology of behavior" to save civilization.

_____. *Walden Two.* New York: The Macmillan Co., 1962. Originally published in 1948, this novel describes what Skinner regards as an ideal society, brought about by the scientific control of human behavior.

Stainback, William C. et al. *Establishing a Token Economy in the Classroom.* Columbus, Ohio: Charles E. Merrill Publishing Co., 1973. Explains in some detail how token economy programs can be implemented.

Ulrich, Roger E. et al. *Control of Human Behavior: Behavior Modification in Education.* Vol. III. Glenview, Illinois: Scott, Foresman and Company, 1974. While the first two volumes of this series are more general, this book of readings focuses on the application of behavior modification in a variety of educational situations.

Williams, Robert L., and Anandam, Kamala. *Cooperative Classroom Management.* Columbus, Ohio: Charles E. Merrill Publishing Co., 1973. Emphasizes the ethical and social aspects of behavior modification and recommends teacher-student cooperation in classroom management.

Index

165

Related Titles

Educational Psychology and Its Classroom Applications
M. Daniel Smith

Behavior Dynamics in Learning, Teaching and Growth
Don E. Hamachek

Educational Psychology, 4th edition
James M. Sawrey and Charles Telford

Contemporary Issues in Educational Psychology, 2nd edition
Harvey F. Clarizio, Robert C. Craig, and William A. Mehrens

Human Dynamics in Psychology and Education,
Selected Readings, 2nd edition
Don E. Hamachek

Objectives for Instruction and Evaluation
*Robert Kibler, Donald J. Cegala, David T. Miles,
and Larry L. Baker*

Teaching/Discipline, 2nd edition
Charles H. Madsen, Jr. and Clifford K. Madsen

Teachers and Learners: The Interactive Process of Education,
2nd edition
Alfred H. Gorman

Human Relations Development: A Manual for Educators
*George M. Gazda, Frank R. Asbury, Fred J. Balzer,
William C. Childers, R. Eric Desselle, and Richard P. Walters*

Helping Relationships: Basic Concepts for the Helping
Professions
Arthur W. Combs, Donald L. Avila, and William W. Purkey

The Helping Relationship Sourcebook
Donald L. Avila, Arthur W. Combs, William W. Purkey

Allyn and Bacon, Inc.
470 Atlantic Ave.
Boston, Mass. 02210

Photo — Anna Kaufman, courtesy of Stock, Boston Inc.

224661